Working with Fiction

WITHDRAWN

Teaching Matters

General Editors: Sydney Hill and Colin Reid

Working with Fiction

by

Mike Hayhoe and Stephen Parker

University of East Anglia

Edward Arnold

© Mike Hayhoe and Stephen Parker 1984

First published 1984
by Edward Arnold (Publishers) Ltd
41 Bedford Square, London WC1B 3DQ

British Library Cataloguing in Publication Data

Hayhoe, Mike
  Working with Fiction.—(Teaching matters)
  1. English language—Studies and teaching
  1. School Libraries
  I. Title   II. Parker, Stephen   III. Series
  420´.7´1   PE1065

  ISBN 0-7131-0935-1

The drawing on p. 48 is by Rosamund Thorne.

Text set in 10/11pt Baskerville by Keyset Composition, Colchester, Essex
Printed in Great Britain at The Pitman Press, Bath

General Editors' Preface

As teachers of English, how many of us can say that we always employ sufficient imagination, knowledge, insight and thought about an activity that rightly claims so much of our time, namely extending children's reading and writing abilities through working with fiction? The authors of this book draw on their wide experience as teachers, observers of classroom practice and teacher-trainers to discuss the role of fiction in the classroom, at home, and in different library settings. They give specific and varied examples of possible ways to help pupils respond to, become involved in and enjoy fiction with a freshness that should stimulate both teacher and taught. They explain how to keep abreast of what is available through organizations, publications and other resources which are concerned with creating a 'positive book climate' in secondary and middle schools, and describe a multi-faceted approach to exploring books through drama, media studies, etc.

In these ways, this particular volume is an excellent example of what the *Teaching Matters* series provides: information and advice on a wide range of educational issues for teachers who are busy, yet who are concerned to keep up to date with new developments.

The aim is practicality: slim volumes that are sources of authoritative help and swift reference, written and edited by people whose expertise in their field is backed up by experience of the everyday realities of school and classroom. The books are planned to cover well-defined topics relevant to schools in widely differing situations: subject teaching, curriculum development, areas of responsibility within schools, and the relationship of the school to the community. They are published at a time when there is a growing call for increased professional accountability in our primary and secondary schools. The 'in-service between covers' that characterizes these handbooks is designed to contribute to the vitality and development of schools and of the individuals within them.

To all the teachers and teachers-in-the-making who have helped us generously over many years.

Contents

1

What this book is about

This book is meant to be brief, to be practical, to be read. It does not set out to be trendy or revolutionary. Based on collaboration with teachers over several years, it aims to present an overview of current practical teaching which promotes active involvement with books. In choosing from its variety of suggestions and developing further ideas of your own, you share in our belief that contact with books is important and should be active and pleasurable.

Most of us have encountered the conventional 'Law Court' approach to literature which expects the reader to argue a case with high skill in a detached way, making constant reference to evidence and comment. 'Macbeth is not entirely evil. Discuss.' invites detailed argument backed by reference and quotation to support one's point of view, all conducted in a scholarly style and an essay format. Such an approach can be deeply rewarding and engrossing, and can lead to further insights into the text and into the reader, but our conversations with teachers suggest that this approach is 'at its best' for the mature and the able. Where it is inappropriate, it may well get in the way of the developing reader. D. W. Harding has argued that our proper business is promoting *feeling comprehension*, in which involvement, response and intellect combine in 'an activity in which we are our own interpretative artist'(1). In 1968 he made the claim that there was too much learning about literature and not enough discriminating enjoyment of it. We believe that the climate has changed and that for many teachers and pupils his hope that literature, rather than literary criticism, would be our proper concern has been largely realized.

That does not mean that reading a book is some sort of literary wallow. Nicholas Tucker talks of 'cognitive dissonance'—of a book being a chance to stretch oneself intellectually as well as emotionally, morally and aesthetically(2). If a book hooks its reader, he or she is not involved in a secondhand experience but a firsthand experience of a particular kind, in which the randomness of the world is given some form through which the reader meets possibilities—of other lifestyles, relationships, situations and values. One's primary world of actuality presents one with life in varied and fluid forms. In the secondary world created by reading, a person encounters the aesthetic as well—the features which have given his or her experience form, which bring about pleasure in what they explore and pleasure in themselves as they create a work of art. This can be seen in anyone who has ever got lost in a book and regrets the leaving of it. 'Reading a book' is far more than mere eye movements across the page. At its best, it involves a genuine, moved interpretation and revision of one's world. Sometimes this is best done in private; sometimes it can be enhanced by a shared celebration of the text.

Much of this book will look at the shared aspect, but it is important to stop here, to stress the point that often the best tactic is to leave the reader and the book alone to get on with their own dialogue. There are many occasions when pupils should be treated as 'ordinary' readers. Ordinary readers do not always talk about what they are reading or have read. When they do, they talk when they are ready, and then informally, 'fixing their reading in the personal and felt mind' as one teacher put it. Just as the individual reader should be left to 'own' his or her reading where it is appropriate, so there are times when 'silence' is the best response to a class reading—that fruitful silence in which to 'do something' with the book would be to trivialize the event and to get in the way. Privacy provides time for reflection, to listen to the inner voice as it comes to terms with the remaking of the pattern which the book has brought about. It may well be that such time for reflection also helps some pupils to consider the art form itself, to become aware of the book's complex patterning and to break out of naïve notions of a book as a linear narrative.

Part of the pleasure to be found in a book lies in responding to it as an experience in itself. A well-told yarn, a finely handled crisis or scene, a well-turned phrase can all please in being so well shaped, just as one gets pleasure from a fine painting or a graceful display of gymnastics. Such pleasure can be found whether a book is happy or sad. Again, there are times when a reader should be allowed to keep this aesthetic pleasure to him/herself.

The variety of approaches which this book describes for shared exploration suggests that involvement makes demands on the head and the heart: for example, a group discussing the creeping tyranny in *Animal Farm* will have to know the text and use it to support points of view; designing a book cover and its blurb demands a very sound knowledge of the book in the first place; writing the 'thoughts in the head' of a character can succeed only when a reader knows the character well and has a sympathetic comprehension of him or her. The importance of this collaboration of sympathy and intelligence needs to be stressed. An author sets out to move the thoughts of a reader in Lawrence's sense of thought—of 'a man in his wholeness wholly attending'. When book and reader meet, the reader engages in 'what if'—what if one is in early love, what if one is suddenly rich or powerful, what if one is alone or misunderstood? In a very serious sense, a reader can explore, can rehearse, can hypothesize, moving from the egocentric into an understanding of the wider reaches of the self, of the possible feelings and stances of others, of the complex nature of relationships. Such an encounter, at its best, is an opportunity for pleasurable learning—and pleasure is the key to reading fiction, reflecting through it and going on reading.

Many teachers set out to promote awareness of the author's craft by engaging the pupils as authors themselves or through other devices. For example, writing an off-stage episode in the author's style or producing a flow-chart of the book's plot or plots can help pupils to see something of the work itself and of its author's intelligence and talents. Becoming aware of an author's qualities in wrestling with a book and shaping it is no bad thing, when such recognition comes through having had to write and criticize and reform one's own efforts as an author has to do.

The work of some of the theoreticians who have informed and enthused us with their advocacy of involvement as the key to entering and harnessing the 'secondary world' of books is to be found in the bibliography(**3**). It is not the proper business of this book to paraphrase their knowledge or their wisdom. Our task has been to suggest that much of what they argue for is already taking place and to bring together this brief recognition of the inventiveness and insight of so much teaching that is going on now. Our hope is that you will find some of the practices it describes already familiar; that you will come across some new ideas; that you will go on to extend the portmanteau of techniques in use and share them with others who see engagement with a book as an active, worthwhile and pleasurable aspect of being alive.

2

Getting and sharing information

One of the main concerns of teachers of English in recent years has been to match pupils and books. Quite often, books from the pre-war and immediate post-war canon still 'work' but increasingly teachers have turned to at least some of the vast current range of children's and young adult fiction available.

'Keeping tabs' on pupils

Perhaps the first priority is to find out about the readers: what and how and why they read—or do not. Clearly this is an area demanding tact and a proper respect for privacy, but there are times when pupils are prepared to share that privacy or when the information is already public.

Personal logs

Some teachers enable pupils to keep personal logs of their travels through a book, whether it is a personally chosen novel or a class reader. They can jot down their feelings as they tackle the book, their views on characters and deeds, their comments on how the book is being handled by the author or by the teacher—whatever seems important to them, for honesty has priority. Such logs are a chance to 'come clean' which may or may not be shared with a teacher.

Borrowers and buyers

Watching how a library is used can provide clues about what is read and how, whether during a timetabled library period or at lunch break. Informal devices include noticing which shelves are used by which age and sex, whether books with cassette introductions or which have had their initial chapters read aloud prove popular, and so on. It is also useful to see whether staff or pupil-recommended books are picked up from thematic, topical, *Just in!* and *These are the tops!* shelves.

More formally, looking at analytical lists can provide information on current tastes, on the tastes of a particular age group or sex. Such lists can arise from looking at the sales returns from the school bookshop or the latest orders for books through a postal buying service. Class library and school library records are also rich sources of information. The personal book reading record set out below is started in the reception year of a high school. Pupils fill in details at some time in every library session and their records travel up the school with them. They write a report on themselves once a year, on the basis of their records, a review activity which they seem to find of considerable interest and some value as they contemplate 'that once was me', looking at their reading tastes and habits and how they have changed. Staff also use the reading records as a basis for 'taking up the child's enthusiasm', as the Bullock Report puts it, through chatting with pupils, bringing together those who have read the same book or who have views to share, and making suggestions about further reading to the pupil who would benefit from advice. The records are also an invaluable source of information for producing advisory reading lists and as background knowledge when buying further stocks. Ideally, records should start in the middle or junior school so that the receiving teacher at secondary level can know something about new pupils: 'So you're Sue Clutterbuck. You're the Sue who likes books about bears, aren't you?'

A High School Personal Reading Record

Netherfell High School	Name										
Reading record	Form		Sheet number								
Title	Author		NF/F	S/O	U/F	1	2	3	4	5

Category: Non-Fiction or Fiction
Source: School or Other source
Completion: Unfinished or Finished
Evaluation: 1 Excellent
2 Good
3 All right
4 Weak
5 Bad

Out of school, sympathetic newsagents, bookshop staff and librarians can provide considerable insight into the reading tastes and styles of young people when they are not being pupils. Their knowledge, allied with your own observation of young people in newsagents, bookshops and libraries, can provide clues about tastes, styles and enthusiasms of which we are not always aware.

In the classroom

Finally, our most frequent site for noting tastes and styles of our pupils remains the classroom. Looking at reactions to texts for class study is a common but difficult activity. In recent years, the increasing use of group study and discussion has helped teachers to be good listeners, and many find time and means for talking with individual readers. This need not only take the usual form of small groups all discussing the same class text. In some schools, classes have access to thematic and genre boxes, containing a range of texts, some as individual copies, some in groups of up to eight. The books also range from the very demanding to the relatively simple. Pupils have been able to make individual or teacher-guided routes through the books available, some reading only one book, some several, depending on such factors as ability and depth of involvement as well as the length and complexity of the books themselves. In observing which books pupils read (or do not) and through tactful, quiet discussion, a teacher can find out much about tastes, problems and enthusiasms and be better equipped to act upon them.

Much of the information a teacher obtains is fluid and cannot be recorded, but where it can be of use to the pupil and be of use to other colleagues it should. Some teachers find it at least worth while to keep jottings on a topic identified at one staff meeting for discussion at another. Others find it more valuable to keep fairly systematic records, sometimes over a considerable period. We still have much to learn about tastes and styles and phases of reading. Intelligent data gathering and pooling of ideas will help in that process.

'Keeping tabs' on books

As for choosing books, relying solely on a literary canon or on nationally produced booklists is not sufficient. It is sad to see how often a nationally or internationally acclaimed book for children sits unvisited on a school library shelf. On the other hand, checking on new books and keeping tabs on what is in vogue is too much of a burden for one teacher—and it is a waste if what he or she does discover is not shared with others. Nicholas Tucker has suggested that schools should pool their insights regionally or locally, and it is well worth considering the opportunities provided by a collaborative approach. For example, a cluster of high schools or a local high school and the middle schools which provide its pupils can arrange to work on a consortium basis, meeting regularly once or twice a term to share information about books, readers and teaching approaches. They can share their pupils' responses to books—and their own. By meeting on a 'circus' basis, they can see others' stocks of library and class books and their working environments. Such groupings of teachers are more likely to be able to afford the shared purchase of *some* of the journals available on children's literature and are more likely to be able to set up development programmes and to attract speakers, consultants and funds(**4**).

The manilla folder

The manilla folder approach can be useful at departmental level. Many publishers still send out catalogues if they are asked for them(**5**). These can be circulated in a folder for staff to tick books that they would like to see bought or borrowed by the school library, bought for class libraries or bought in for bookshop stock. An equally important approach involves individuals 'adopting' a paper or periodical and circulating its reviews and articles on pupils' reading and on children's and young adult fiction. The head of department might adopt *The Times Educational Supplement*; others such daily and Sunday papers as *The Guardian, The Telegraph, The Times* and *The Observer*, as well as such journals as *The New Statesman*.

Specialist journals

Larger English departments may still have the funds to buy some of the specialist journals on children's books and their reading, but some smaller schools may not. The collaborative approach can turn poverty into an opportunity, with schools pooling funds to buy at least some of the journals and using their circulation as an opportunity for English staff to meet and discuss points in articles and their own views and findings. Journals come and journals go, but there are four basic types:

a) general journals on English, with some articles on classroom practice, e.g. *English in Education* and *The Use of English*;

b) general journals on children's literature, with occasional articles on classroom practice, e.g. *Children's Literature in Education, Signal* and *Growing Point*;

c) journals on private reading provision in libraries, e.g. *The School Librarian* and through school bookshops, e.g. *Books for Keeps*;

d) material specifically reviewing books for classroom use and identifying possible teaching tactics, e.g. *Bookpage*(**6**).

On a realistic note, it is worth each school buying one journal, so that it has an interest in getting it back. A journal can get lost where no particular school or individual regards it as its property!

Wider sharing

Some parts of the country are lucky enough to have English advisers or teachers' centres or a branch of NATE, The National Association for the Teaching of English. LEA or NATE meetings can bring together a wide range of teachers and may be able to afford the occasional well-known speaker. Some public libraries offer facilities for meetings on children's and young adult fiction which involve anyone who is interested—teachers, librarians, parents, booksellers and sometimes the clients themselves. One progressive city bookshop runs a highly successful annual Book Fair, attracting from across the county all those interested in children's fiction. The daytime is given over to pupils, who encounter books *en masse*, varied entertainment, authors and artists—all providing a fine chance for adults to see who likes what. The evening events are for adults providing time to listen to speakers and to share observations, views, and possibilities for the future.

Finally, there are courses and conferences on fiction for children and adolescents, at local, regional and national levels. National events attract big names and are a splendid opportunity to meet people, to browse through hosts of the latest books and to come back to school laden with catalogues for the manilla folder and posters and book covers for the library. Regional events are a powerful means of pooling actual experience and finding out what does work in the area. In both cases, it is worth trying to send two people rather than one, if the budget will bear it. On a smaller scale, the sector or inter-school day conference has much to offer, looking at such topics as schools' bookstocks and buying criteria; which books are used at what age and how and why; library policy and use; bookshop provision and liaison inside and outside the schools; techniques for keeping tabs on pupils' reading phases, tastes, styles. From such a day can come a series of further meetings within and across schools, leading to a fuller knowledge of what is available and of who might read it, enjoy it and grow because of it.

All of these suggestions can be handled lightly, but they also need some element of organization if they are not to fade away. Documents for circulation should be passed on to the next reader by a certain date, for example. Certainly there should be some sort of record of meetings. There should be written reports of courses and conferences. Wherever there is inquiry or information to be shared, it should not be allowed to vanish in the air but should appear, however succinctly, in print for others to refer to and to learn from. Getting, sharing and reflecting on information about readers and their reading is the essential basis for any work on the theme of this book.

3

Creating a positive book climate

In a talk he gave to a meeting of student teachers about getting pupils to read, Aidan Chambers suggested that a teacher is a curious mixture of disciple and enthusiast. Teachers, simply by being seen to be keen and rewarded readers, show that books can offer much, including pleasure. There are times when a touch of the salesman's zest does not come amiss in suggesting a book and saying, 'Read this. You'll love it!'

Clearly, the disciple-enthusiast can do much in the classroom, but Aidan Chambers is quite right in suggesting that his or her efforts will not get very far if the school does not provide a wider, supportive 'reading climate'. Without our suggesting any sort of priority among them, there are devices which can help to make books and the reading of them seem natural and pleasurable.

Borrowing books: the school library

It is interesting to notice how department stores sell goods with special promotions, advertising campaigns, moving stock into prominent positions for a while, harnessing personalities—and so on. Similar techniques can have their place in helping to make a library a lively and attractive place, without cheapening it.

Book displays—staff choice

It can be a good idea to make a display of books in a particular genre. One high school department uses westerns as a lead into genre study in its third year—an excellent opportunity for the library to display its range of westerns and its non-fiction on 'Out West' as a special item in a prominent shelf area. There are other opportunities for special, temporary display, for example books on a topic which a form or a year is working on; books by an author who is visiting or who has visited the school; books which 'fit' a popular television series. All of these suggest an alert, aware library helping to bring stock to pupils' (and teachers') attention. Something to remember is that these small, selective displays provide a chance to show books' covers rather than their spines, or even to show some inside pages. Both of these are far more efficient lures to the casual browser who may find the information on spines to be cryptic, just as he or she may find the overabundance of books in the library as a whole confusing and demoralizing.

Many school libraries exploit the attractiveness of new stock by having a *New!* or *Just in!* shelf in a prominent position. Some invest in special display equipment, including spotlights. A display need not only be visual: reading an exciting chunk to a form and leaving it at a cliff-hanger moment can often help to promote a book very effectively. Some schools produce selective lists of recommendations, in the spirit of the Bullock Report's notion of supported individualized reading. These may be as simple as lists of new books. The most helpful are probably those on a genre, theme or subject—westerns, survival, horses—which contain brief, introductory comments to help pupils make an initial choice from a sample of between a dozen and thirty books.

Book displays—pupil choice

Pupils can certainly be used to create any of the displays already suggested; a sensible, purposeful discussion session can arise from a class working out which books it proposes to put on display as its choice on a topic or within a genre, when the display has a large sign acknowledging its selectors. Some forms enjoy being used as critics and book 'pushers' as they select their personal choice for a recommendations shelf and design its presentation. A shelf in one library entitled *These are the goods!* puts that in a much more lively way. In some schools, each form has a *recommendations book* in which pupils can write comments about books; it may be that recommendations cards would be a better idea, since an index system could be used. In one instance, pupils stick stars on the spines of books, the colour of a star relating to the pupil's year. A maximum of five stars ensures that the spine's information does not become completely hidden and signals that the book is likely to be a particularly good read. Those teachers who believe that girls value different books from boys might like to experiment with two shapes, perhaps—circles for boys and stars for girls—to see if there is evidence of different tastes and enthusiasms. The brave might like to try a graffiti pinboard or whiteboard on which readers can put their (signed?) comments on books to enthuse or warn others!

Advertising

Anyone who has used the Schools Council *Language in Use* project will recall unit B9 on advertising, in which pupils produce their own advertising campaign. Some interesting English lessons can grow out of getting a form to produce advertising for a reading or book club or library campaign. The poster in one school declaring *You're better in bed with a book!*

still comes to mind, as does *Get lost—with a book*. It is also worth persuading art colleagues to work on book design with pupils, so that they design alternative covers for books they have enjoyed. This means that everyone in a class has to read a book, has to justify his or her design, and has the satisfaction of seeing the book using that cover for a special display in the library. With a proper write-up, such work can lure some parents away from the canoes on Parents' Evening to look at some English work, for a change!

'Beach-head' cassettes

The early pages of a novel or short story are the hardest. The reader meets more information more rapidly than elsewhere in the work and at the same time has to crack the author's style, establish relationships with characters, get the gist of the plot and its potential lines forward, and a great deal more. For less able and less confident readers, the early pages can be a great problem. Some schools have found that they have helped some pupils to establish a beach-head by putting on to cassette tape the first one or two chapters, so that they can follow the story visually and aurally for a while. A book which has an accompanying cassette has a special sticker on it, to show the cassette number, and pupils can ask for the cassette at the issue desk as a companion to the book when they take it out.

It is worth making your own tapes where copyright rules allow or considering Hertfordshire Library's *Starter Tapes*. The range of professionally produced tapes is greater than some schools may realize, and many of them are very good indeed(7). One school has invested in a *listening centre* in its library where books, cassettes and cassette players are available as a private reading opportunity, attracting not only the less able pupil but the more sophisticated who enjoy, for example, Claire Bloom's reading of *Pride and Prejudice*.

The visiting reader

There are many fine readers in a school staffroom and beyond. It can be worth inviting them to read their favourite short story or chunk from a favourite novel for, say, fifteen minutes during a lunchtime open library session. Provided that you choose your readers well and can alert them to choose fiction which amuses or enthralls or makes an audience shudder or be gently moved, such sessions, held regularly, tend to grow in popularity especially in the colder months of the year. Some schools use the regional arts associations' facilities for bringing in a local author who will come to a library period and read and talk about his or her work(8). There is something about an author walking to a shelf in a library and picking up a book and saying that it is *his* book.

Play it again

Beware of the copyright laws but where it is legally possible, use radio and television versions of books as lures to read further and as part of a library's literary facilities. Pupils may have missed a broadcast for many reasons, and presenting a series during lunch breaks can be a good means of linking broadcasting and reading as approved activities. *Books for Keeps* and *The School Librarian* give early information on forthcoming television versions of novels so that you can engage in preparatory and follow-up work—and ensure that copies of the book are available in the library or the bookshop.

Floppy areas

Most library seating arrangements seem more concerned with deport-ment than attentiveness. Doubtless some people read best when on a fairly hard, upright seat, with a desk or table to rest a book on—and this is certainly a fine setting for study. Relaxed reading, on the other hand, usually involves physical relaxation as well. Some middle schools have a carpeted area, old cushions, even old arm-chairs, which form a floppy area. One secondary school has invested in 'sag bags' for its library. It could be that judicious and well-supervised moves towards such an area would attract some pupils who find the more formal climate unattractive.

Borrowing books—the class library

Clearly many of the suggestions for a school library will apply to class libraries as well, but class libraries also have other strengths. Because their stocks are smaller, some pupils may feel that they are more manageable. The smaller stock also makes it more likely that several pupils will have read or tried to read the same book. As a result they have a shared literary experience to talk about and, sometimes, to work from. If a class library stock is based on informed choice, it can provide a sensible, attractive and accessible core of fiction from which pupils can grow into the greater stock of the school library.

Paperbacks, please!

Class libraries provide a good opportunity to use paperbacks. Because they are cheaper, stock can change a little more rapidly than when relying on hardbacks. Probably more important is the fact that some pupils are more at ease with paperbacks. This may be because their covers can be more attractive, but the more likely reason is that such bindings do not instil the awe of hardbacks, which some see as 'posh', for 'them', or, as one pupil put it, 'Hardbacks must be hard'. Clear, sticky-backed plastic sheeting obtainable from stationers, or plastic covers obtainable from library supply firms, extend the life of paperbacks considerably.

Sh! I'm reading!

Class libraries can help to make an unusual contribution to a school's reading climate. In one high school, teachers and pupils alike take time to settle down for a good read every day for half an hour after lunch. Users of this approach to reading claim that the impact on the school's ethos has been very favourable; that people's language skills have improved; that the experience has helped to increase concentration and to introduce a time of quiet pleasure. This certainly follows the Bullock Report's advocacy of time for individual reading being a component of the school week. As the Bradford Book Flood project showed, the provision of regular quiet reading time is a crucial factor in promoting interest in reading books and providing the length of time and stillness in which reflective reading can grow**(9)**. An essential point is that *teachers* should settle down to some reading alongside their pupils.

Class club libraries

Only a few schools run these, but they are worth considering. Members of a form agree to contribute a small sum on a regular basis. Five pence a week per pupil can raise five or six pounds every four weeks. Over the course of a year, all of the club's members have a session on its committee, sorting out by discussion and interview and by visits to a bookshop the next paperbacks to buy for the club library. It is possible to have two or three committees during a term, each committee having to present and justify its choice of new books to the full club. Such an exercise leads to some careful reading and some very concentrated discussion on the part of the pupils. It is wise to make friends with a local bookseller, to be aware that committee meetings and book-buying expeditions are likely to eat into your time, and that you may have to vet the occasional book suggestions, but pupils like the sense of responsibility such a library provides. Again, each pupil should have a plastic cover in which to protect borrowed texts. The library can be dismantled at the end of the year by letting pupils choose volumes to keep, or by lottery, or by selling books at a quarter of the original price, the money helping to prime the next club library.

Buying books

The school bookshop

The best motivator for reading a book may be having laid out good money for it. A school bookshop can be one means of building the habit of investing money and reading time in books. It is well worth seeking the detailed, expert advice of the School Bookshop Association and of a friendly local bookseller**(10)**. School bookshops need to be in a bright, central area. This need not necessarily be in a library: a school's reception area or somewhere en route to the dining hall can be useful. Stock needs to be small and changing, for it must not 'drag'. Booksellers and other colleagues will be invaluable sources of information on what is likely to sell, and it is worth keeping a record of which books do move quickly. Bags and bookmarks help to make a purchase more authentic—you've really bought a book. Posters from publishers or from pupils help to make the bookshop more lively, and can provide information about authors, genres, and new publications. Some schools provide a table for a bookshop; some have had bookshops designed and built by senior pupils as a CSE project. Whatever the options, bookshops can prove an attraction. In one school bookshop, books can be sold back in good condition for a third of the original price and put back on sale at a half. The bargain hunters find it hard to resist such lures.

Book clubs

It may not be possible or advisable to run a bookshop for some reason, but many schools use the postal bookclubs run by several firms**(11)**. It is worth exploiting the opportunities these provide: simply to issue and accept order forms and to issue books is not enough. When the order forms appear, it can be worth getting pupils to vet titles by finding and reading other books by an author or by looking at other books on the same topic as a listed book. This can lead to reporting back by the vetting groups and more informed discussion and decision-making about which books to buy. It is certainly no bad idea to make book arrival day a special occasion and to drop a lesson or part of it so that pupils can start reading, if they want to. A later session can have pupils reporting back on the books they bought and discussing how far the blurb on the order form, and their expectations, were fulfilled when they actually came to read their choice.

Out and about or coming in

Getting pupils out to see the greater book environment or getting people to come into school to talk about it can help them to realize that books and reading are not only school business.

Libraries

Some children are used to public libraries; many are not. It seems a sensible investment to make a series of visits to local public libraries, working out a programme with the librarians in which pupils come to see libraries as quiet but welcoming places and come to understand the people and systems which will help them to tap their rich resources. 'One off' visits do not prove very successful: it is regular visits and familiarity which bring about the early habit of using libraries. In some instances, librarians will come to the school for a brief series of preparatory sessions working alongside a teacher, so that pupils know a familiar face and something of the public library before their first visit. It is worth remembering that librarians are usually better read than we are. In particular, children's and youth librarians have a vast personal knowledge, based on the reading of many hundreds of books for these age ranges and on their needing to keep up with current publications, reviews and tastes. (There can be up to three thousand new children's fiction texts a year.) Such people are keen to help in the process of bridging the use of school and public libraries. They are well worth consulting.

Printers

Seeing how a book is made can be fascinating. Ideally, a visit to a printer's shows the complex organization and processes involved, but not all will allow schoolchildren round their works. In some cases a printer will send a speaker, complete with visual aids, to a school. In either instance, pupils may get slightly more respect for books and not commit the ultimate sin of bending them back!

Authors

Long before the printer sets to work on it, a book has been made by its author. Regional arts associations and some publishers have lists of writers who will visit schools to talk or work with pupils on their own fiction and that of the pupils(12). Some like to run a writer's workshop for half a day with pupils; others are prepared to sit for an afternoon in a library and talk with small groups or pairs or individuals about work which they have sent to him or her beforehand. Some authors show their audiences how they came to write a story, explaining what was put in and what was left out. One particular author, John Gordon, has taken classes along the route of his novel *The House on the Brink*, following the river to the house at the novel's centre, using the opportunity to discuss how he wrote about it as he did and to see how his travelling companions see the places and how they might use them in stories of their own. Seek advice along the grapevine of other teachers, the library and advisory services in your area about the most accessible and flexible writers available. At their best, they have great impact on pupils of all ages and stages of sophistication.

Parents

There are parents who read books and talk about them with their children and who have created a home climate in which it is natural for children to read books and, sometimes, to talk about them with their parents. Not all homes provide such a climate: some parents do not read and some are not aware of what their children might read. Most of the tactics schools have adopted to promote reading affect only those parents who turn up at school evening sessions, but they are still worth using. These can include specific, age-related displays of books set out for a particular parents' evening; a reading consultancy stall; annotated booklists for particular age ranges; having the bookshop open. One school has a book fair in November with visiting speakers, films, and a bookstall run by a local bookshop. The two-day event is seen as a special occasion, with quizzes and raffles and a generally festive air during day and evening sessions, the idea being to sell the idea of books for Christmas. Clearly such an event can also provide a chance for the pupils to display their work as well— their stories, reviews, posters, and bookjackets; their dramatizations and illustrations; their reading records and surveys of reading habits— including those of their parents! More direct methods will not necessarily be more effective, but some schools send out to parents lists of books which pupils might find at their level in a particular year; some send out a year's fiction 'syllabus' with brief commentary on the texts. In some instances, children borrow books from the school library for their parents, since their parents feel unsure of public libraries or become interested in what their children are reading. It seems good sense to encourage this practice, where possible: it is exciting when a pupil sets out to hook someone else on books.

4

Reading—quietly

It is probably true to say that most books are written to be read privately so that the reader can make his or her own meaning from them. The importance of this quiet, individual approach cannot be stressed too much. As Dr. Johnson put it, 'A man ought to read just as inclination leads him', for in private reading the reader has the greatest chance of bringing himself or herself to the book without other people getting in the way. Much of the rest of this book sets out techniques for helping students to make public what they bring to the act of reading; this section sets out some of the ways of helping to develop the reader as a 'bringer' on his own.

Reading—frequently

It is certainly a good idea to make it clear that reading on one's own is a sensible, 'ordinary' thing to do. Given school and class libraries, and an easy issuing system, there is no reason why students should not be expected to carry a book with them—and no reason why that book should not be read where there is time for it. Time *needs* to be found, as the Bradford Book Flood showed, for without it a school fails to provide the quiet climate in which book and pupil may meet. Such time can be official—as part of a library lesson or an English lesson—but there can be many other opportunities for it to be read. Ideally, the library or a quiet area should be available during lunch break for those who want to read. It is also worth considering having such a place open before school and after. That means a lot of extra supervision, but it can also provide some of those quiet moments of the day which some pupils may not find elsewhere, either in school or at home. Some colleagues may agree to pupils having their books with them in other subjects, so that if there are a few minutes to spare somewhere in a lesson they can be spent reading.

Reading can also be used as a means of reducing a teacher's load. In one school, assignment sheets have been worked out for a wide range of books, the tasks starting with a few test items to ensure that the book has been read but going on to allow the pupil to do his or her own work in interpreting the book and writing on from it. Using such a device, a teacher can hive off some pupils to work along these lines for a week or so and concentrate on others in the class—and then swap the pupils over for the following week. With due preparation, this technique can help to break the burden of having to work with a whole class and can give pupils the chance to work solo on a book for a slightly extended and intensive period.

Reading—widely

Ideally, extending the range of what is read should grow from pupils and staff sharing their enthusiasms, tastes and insights. Where staff have managed to produce a range of assignments along the lines just suggested, some pupils can be gently obliged to read more widely, perhaps sampling texts in genres they have not considered before, such as science fiction and historical novels. Width needs to be seen in terms of ability as well as interest, and ensuring that books match and stretch their readers is no easy task. Most readability measures are too crude to be appropriate in assessing what sort of book will suit which child. It is probably more appropriate to think of the pupils instead. 'What interests them?' must come first, for motivation is the main key to reading. Other factors are their experience, their language development and their skill in tackling literary conventions. It is worth keeping simple checklists of this sort so that pupils are not introduced to texts which are inappropriate or inadequate.

Training for independence

Not all teachers will want to provide a limited selection of books for pupils to work from, although this is defended by some as a means of introducing children to a guided choice in what otherwise might seem a bewildering and demoralizing plethora of books. Certainly pupils should move on from such lists. This development will come about if steps are taken to ensure that pupils are familiar with the structure of a book, so that they know about the clues which are provided by its title, its blurb, any critics' reviews, its chapter titles and its illustrations. Many pupils do not know the siting of some of these items within a book but it is worth taking the time to teach them where they are and to run a few brief exercises in scanning a book for its possibilities as a good read. Looking at title, blurb, reviews, chapter titles and illustrations, pupils can present a quick summary to others or make a brief jotting for themselves about the information and expectations they have gained. From such a preliminary outline, some readers are likely to read on with something of a map of the book inside their minds and hence approach it with greater confidence.

Some readers believe that every word in a work of fiction is to be read. For those who hold strongly to such a view, the following comments may seem like sacrilege, but we make no apologies for them. A novel calls upon a range of techniques, all of which may well be experienced by a mature reader, but it should not be expected that this should be the case with every text, especially when it is being read on the reader's own terms, as a private event. For example, young readers are more likely to respond to the pace of a story's narrative and to characters in terms of their actions than to elaborate settings of scene or mood and to extended musings on the part of the hero or heroine. They are more likely to value dialogue when it is crisp, is clearly labelled with the name of the speakers and is supported by authorial comment on what is going on. Page after page of dialogue in which characters are not identified and the action or mood is implied are far more difficult to cope with. In such circumstances as these, early readers are quite likely to skip bits until they find a passage further on in the book which they can cope with. 'Skipping' should be recognized as a natural response to a book: it may well be better for a pupil to have skipped through a book and gained some achievement in it than to have ploughed virtuously through two or three chapters and then given up. Pupils should be encouraged to keep brief notes on the 'bits' they have enjoyed working through slowly and which they have skipped, for these notes can prove a useful basis for informed and informal discussion between teacher and pupil about features within fiction and features of the reader's tastes and abilities which will repay further attention.

Skipping has one further advantage. One of the important features of books is that they can invite being visited more than once. There is no harm in signalling to pupils that 're-visitation' can be pleasurable and interesting, in order to see how the book and its reader have changed. Skipping can sometimes be the first reading; sometimes it can be the device for the re-visitation. In senior forms, it can be a means by which pupils, working in pairs, take on one or two new books each and present reviews to their own class or to other forms, so that information about the quality and suitability of texts comes from pupils as well as from busy teachers!

Ways in

A library is a source of bewilderment to many pupils, with its vast numbers of books and the curious way in which they are arranged. Alphabetical order by author's name may well be logical to an adult mind, but to the insecure reader who has a slight interest in books to do with school or with horses or people getting lost or children becoming orphaned and having to survive, it makes very little sense indeed. Colleagues can save each other a great deal of work by adopting a theme each—horses, growing up, sea stories, survival, ghosts, living in the country, westerns, silly stories, outer space—and producing for each topic brief details of books which make a good read. These should include the title, the author, publisher and catalogue details, and a brief description of the book's content and likely appeal. These can be produced as A4 duplicated sheets or as a suitably organized card-index system. Children will use this sort of catalogue or suggestions list where the general Dewey or alphabetical system causes them to shy away. It is therefore worth developing, in spite of the effort it involves. Ideally, liaison with other schools and the local children's or youth librarian should result in a collaborative effort which goes beyond a single school, with everyone's ideas being pooled. As a time-saving device, one or two schools find the details and blurb provided in some publishers' catalogues is generally reliable and adequate, and these are cut out and pasted on cards for their thematic card-index system. One or two publishers' catalogues contain thematic lists**(13)**. The Junior Fiction Index, with its thematic approach, is another useful point from which to start**(14)**.

Providing entry

Some pupils will pick up a book with the best intention in the world but find it hard to get through the barrier of its first two or three chapters. In some cases, an oral or written summary of the first hurdle by the teacher may be enough to help them move on; in some, having a beach-head cassette can prove helpful. In some cases, the teacher may be able to consult records and see that some other pupil has read the book and use him or her as the means of helping by chatting informally with the book's new reader, if they get on with one another.

Thinking about it

The personal, individual response of the reader should be the concern of teacher and pupil alike, whether the pupil is in the first year or in a senior form facing a public examination. While examiners and teachers decry model answers which have been learned parrot-fashion, some have traditionally rejected the highly subjective response, particularly from older pupils, of the 'I thought this was marvellous' or the 'This reminded me of when' kind. There may be arguments for its exclusion in a public examination, but it is central at all stages and ages in developing a full, exploratory response to books and ourselves as readers. In a serious sense, we tend to gossip about books. They affect us. We often relate them to our own experience. We often reflect upon the effect they have had upon us and our view of the world by chatting about them. If adults engage in such activities, they cannot be labelled as 'immature', to be relegated to the younger forms and the less able.

Talk will often be the most immediate and natural means of promoting such gossip. Sometimes, however, it may put off the shy. Sometimes such response is forgotten. Sometimes, the gossip may be internal.

Another device is the personal log, described in greater detail in *Chapter 8*. Through keeping a personal commentary on the process of engaging with a book, pupils have a chance to understand something of their own task as reader as well as something of the tasks of the author. The ideal log enables its compiler to see how he or she has changed during encounters with a book, recognizing how skills and attitudes have been challenged and have grown, seeing how sometimes a reader and a book fail to make a relationship and how sometimes they do. Keeping a log can be onerous. Sometimes it pays off, helping a reader to see his or her increasing competence and maturity as a reader of books and as one who reflects on the ways of the world.

5

Exploring through talk

Talking is often our most immediate way of sharing. The first story tellers talked their stories to other people, and certainly a good raconteur attracts an audience with ease. Alongside this comes the natural activity of passing comment on a tale—a word of praise or criticism or 'That reminds me of'. A lot of the celebration and exploration of a book can—and often should—come about through talk.

Putting language in children's ears

Reading is often a private and silent act which we should make as frequent, as natural and as rewarding as possible. There are occasions, however, where there is something to be said for a reading out loud. A good reading might almost be called celebratory: it does the book justice, it engrosses at least some of the pupils and it displays the reader's acting skills. In other words, reader and audience can get pleasure from a good reading out loud.

The teacher as reader

Many teachers read to their classes with enthusiasm and skill and do not stop reading as their pupils move up the school. Fairly frequent reading, whether on a regular or irregular basis, provides a grand chance to range widely across novels and stories. While showing pupils the vast variety of material available to be enjoyed, there is more to such an activity than mere coverage. A good reader acts. Without being melodramatic, his or her voice changes in pitch, tone and timbre as character or situation suggest; the face changes; shoulders hunch into a looming shape for a giant and slope for the despair of the hero in Kafka's *Metamorphosis*; a hand rises slightly and sways hypnotically as Kaa, the python, works on the monkeys in Kipling's *The Jungle Book*. The result is akin to theatre as the book performs itself through its intelligent, experienced, prepared reader—and the pupils experience something of the potential of a text when it is interpreted in this active way. This applies whether a complete book is being read or a series of 'tasters'—episodes from books to entice pupils to read more widely.

Often that is enough. As Gabriel Josipovici has suggested, there are two things that a book can call upon us to do—to respond with *silence* or to respond through *game* (**15**). A book makes many demands on its audience: there is a unique linguistic style to understand; characters to become involved with; issues to consider; aesthetics to begin to appreciate—and so on. There are times when it is essential that the story be left to do its own work in silence—when to talk about it or write about it would, at the very least, diminish its effect. The class itself usually provides the signals—a quiet attentiveness, a reflective mood suggesting that they are busy coming to terms with the tale's experience and that to intrude would be unwise as they engage in an internal dialogue with the story. Such occasions may be uncommon, but they should be watched for and valued. The eager teacher who wants every story discussed or used can actually inhibit response if such occasions for privacy are invaded.

The rest of this book looks at the range of games that can sometimes be played back at a book. Certainly, reading out loud is a kind of game. It is worth remembering that language in prose fiction is not the same as everyday language. It is likely to be more shaped and to have to carry far more than ordinary language by way of characterization, plot structure hints, and so on. That has implications for reading, as can the length or complexity of a work. Dickens used to be quite ruthless in presenting his novels, editing them severely for his famed public readings. It could be that we should be equally bold with some of our reading out loud sessions, so that the story has a chance to live in a slim form when it is read out loud, leaving its fuller version for those who want to make the book their own by private, silent, more leisurely reading.

Only the teacher can decide when to celebrate a text in its entirety or when to edit it in some way. 'Skipping' can be achieved by a range of devices, including:

a) compressing or omitting passages of extended description, authorial comment or character 'philosophizing';
b) linking passages with a summarizing commentary;
c) editing out 'minutiae', leaving a framework of key sentences with some filling out from the text;
d) substituting for difficult vocabulary. Some teachers prefer to *expand* the text at such points, slipping in further clues so that pupils will grasp the meaning—for example, slipping in a synonym alongside or commenting 'That is to say . . .' within the reading itself.

Only the teacher can decide another issue—whether all the class are expected to listen to a story or whether people can opt out. Ideally, perhaps, a reading should involve everyone. If it does not, some teachers find it useful to let some pupils 'contract' into some quiet reading instead.

The pupils as readers

Practice is very mixed as far as this activity is concerned. Some teachers view 'reading round the class' with certain misgivings, arguing that bright children may be slowed up and slow readers embarrassed. What should be a celebration of a text can sometimes seem like a wake and a basic literacy test combined. Other teachers disagree and find that pupils enjoy volunteering to read and having their moment of owning the class and its attention, no matter how poor a reader a particular pupil may be. Some teachers provide class or homework time for pupils to prepare their chunk before the reading out loud session. Some do not find that these private rehearsals improve the quality of the reading and believe that they spoil the spontaneity of discovering the text as it is being read out.

One way round this is to have pairs or small groups present an episode from a story. This might be the start of a book or a moment of crisis. It might be a particularly descriptive passage, such as the hero's encounter with the dawn garden in Philippa Pearce's *Tom's Midnight Garden* (chapter 5) or, for older pupils, the unsuccessful sea rescue in chapter 51 of *David Copperfield*. Most accessible of all is an episode involving extensive dialogue. One group of Heads of English has suggested that it finds few good plays for reading round the lower secondary school classroom, because their techniques of characterization and dialogue have to be made obvious in order to provide young readers with adequate clues on how to interpret their parts(**16**). They suggest that novels with lots of dialogue in them—and lots of clues and comment about characters, their moods and relationships—are much more accessible to young readers. Such books can act as play scripts with extensive stage directions as readers learn to adjust their voices to the people, places and atmospheres they are trying to interpret and present as a group activity to others. *The Pinballs* by Betsy Byars and Nicholas Fisk's *Trillions* and *High Way Home* are examples of books which teachers have found useful for this purpose.

There are teachers who ask small groups to find an episode and to go away and prepare it for presentation on cassette tape, sometimes complete with sound effects. One school has found that parents will listen to such tapes on an open evening when they simply pass by written work. Another has sent tapes to lower forms and to a junior school, for presentations along the lines of *Jackanory*—and the fact that such readings are to have a genuine audience makes the discussion and interpretation which go into their preparation all the more motivated and genuine.

Listening

It is often said that pupils do too much listening in schools; but listening to stories is certainly justified both educationally and for the pleasure it can often provide. Listening to the teacher as storyteller is one example, although this book has already suggested that listening to other teachers and to 'outsiders' can widen the range of styles of presentation which the pupils encounter—and the range of tastes and materials as well. Some firms produce cassettes of stories. Certainly, it is worth recording many of the BBC schools radio broadcasts involving story, listening to them yourself, and presenting those which you think your pupils might enjoy. It is usually worth getting hold of the teachers' notes to such series. Programmes change, but *Inside Pages*, *Adventure Stories*, *CSE English* and *Books, Plays, Poems* are examples of useful series.

Getting members of a class or group to listen to peers' presentations may well need some preparation, including insisting on the groundrule that any criticism should be courteous and should be about achievements rather than imperfections.

Listening to an author can be very effective. Some simply read from a book of their own or from books which they like; some will read and explain the struggles they have had in shaping and reshaping a paragraph, even a sentence; some will explain carefully how they planned a story. Use the local grapevine to find out which local authors are worth inviting; then use your local Arts Association to help finance their visit to your school or cluster of schools.

Informal talk

Making an agenda

Talking about a story can be a fine way of finding out what sort of agenda is going to be worth following up in the text. It is certainly worth running an informal swap shop from time to time, in which a story or part of a story is read simply to see if such material is going to be suitable for the class. A casual 'Were there any bits you liked or didn't like in that?' may lead into a few minutes' profferings and discussion of a relaxed kind and may even enable you to join in with the occasional 'I liked that bit when . . .'. Where such a climate can be brought about, gossiping about books is seen as something as natural as chatting about football or a disco—and can be built on**(17)**.

Linking with the world

Whatever their ability, pupils link books to their lives and the lives of those close to them, just as they test their lives against a book's characters and the challenges and opportunities they encounter. Such linking is most likely to come about in free discussion, perhaps with the teacher keeping in the background, but there are other devices. One secondary school, for example, uses Nina Bawden's *Carrie's War* as a class reader with its reception year pupils. They do simple research in the library about what life was like in the dim and distant days of World War II and find out from relatives and friends anecdotes about civilian life in those times. This has led to their re-telling experiences that they have heard or read. As a class, they have collaborated among themselves and with other generations to produce a context in which the book can live (see p. 42). Similar work has been done on local novels, for example Hester Burton's *The Great Gale* and its tale of the 1953 East Anglian floods. Through reporting back from television and press coverage and some personal contacts, work on more contemporary novels, such as Joan Lingard's books on the Irish troubles, has been given more immediate point.

Linking with other art forms
Books can also be linked to other books and art forms. It can be very interesting to compare a radio or theatre version of a story with its original and to chat about similarities and differences. The same can be done with television versions and film interpretations. Some teachers have asked pupils to find pictures which might fit. In both cases, there is bound to be some talk about the story itself.

Book pushing
An earlier section suggested ways of getting pupils to become book critics, organizing displays of books for the library or class library, designing posters and advertising campaigns, helping to run book clubs and book-shops and discussing books they have bought. There are many more chances for pupils to discuss and report on books when they are actively engaged in the process of promoting them.

Offering guidance—structured talk

Teacher questions

Any experienced teacher will already be skilled in questioning, but it may be worth reconsidering the potential of some of the techniques available and their appropriateness. For example, which questions to ask pupils to consider depends on the text being looked at and the abilities and climate of the class, but there are some general principles which might be useful. The most straightforward approach to questioning considers three main types: closed, open and enabling.

Closed questions expect a specific answer. 'How old was Oliver Twist when he was farmed out to the branch workhouse?' is an example. Closed questions may not stimulate wide-ranging discussion but they can have a place in getting pupils to refer to the text in order to discuss possible answers and share advice on where to look for information, especially when the answer is not explicit in the text.

Open questions involve values and judgments. 'Was Oliver justified in picking pockets?' is an example. There is no right answer; such questions expect discussion. They are one of the most important devices open to a teacher, for the pupils are being asked to compare experiences and values in their reading with others in their own lives. Such questioning does not always get a ready answer—or a deep one—but it is worth persevering with.

Enabling questions prompt pupils to explore their ideas further. 'Why did you think that?' and 'Is there any further comment we can make on X at this stage?' are examples. Such promptings can elicit factual information from the text or impressions, value judgments or hypotheses. They are useful in expanding pupils' thinking as a component of their personal response to the text and developing greater reflectiveness. The Bullock Report quoted C. S. Lewis's remark, 'Nothing, I suspect, is more astonishing in any man's life than the discovery that there do exist people very, very like himself.' Skilled, tactful questioning can sometimes be used to further this insight through reflecting on the links between literature and pupils' lives.

Group discussion

Discussion between the teacher and the whole class is one kind of participation, but it is very demanding. Most pupils speak only if they are not going to be laughed at, and from the point of view of time alone, very few people can speak during a lesson. Thirty pupils in a generous double period of ninety minutes will have under three minutes' talk time each. There is a need to exploit the opportunities provided by group work, through subdividing the class into groups of varying sizes. Again, group work is easy for an experienced teacher to handle with an experienced class, but there are times when it is worth moving very slowly.

As with any technique, pupils may need some training in what is expected of them, especially since there will be a lot of talking going on at the same time and most classrooms are acoustic nonsenses. Setting out an explicit specification of what is allowed in group work; outlining clearly what is to be discussed, for how long, with what and how many outcomes; and making control the focus of your attention for the first two or three briefish discussion sessions can all help to settle matters down.

The next issue is how pupils talk to one another. They do not always discuss fiction in an *extended* way outside the classroom and some may need guidance on how to react to others' viewpoints—how to be supportive, to be critical without jeering, to maintain a sense of direction and how to sum up the group's viewpoint or viewpoints. Sophisticated groups can do all of these; beginners may value having an agenda of items to track down in a text and then to discuss and report back on. Try also getting pupils to proffer their *own* questions for the class to work from(**18**).

Such agendas can be questions on the board, an assignment sheet or oral instructions. The clearer they are, especially in the early stages, the more likely it is that the noise levels will be acceptable, that pupils will work constructively and that they will maintain impetus. It is usually sensible to spell out your expectations about the time allowed, the area to be explored and the results to be expected, for example, 'You have five minutes now to consider the two main ways in which the main character is being deceitful in this chapter. Working with your partner, jot down what you think they are. Then jot down the actions which make you think this, with page references, since we'll need these for the next stage, when we'll discuss your findings as a class.' The slight sense of pressure which a time limit induces can help to motivate pupils, although some groups may need help to cope. Knowing what is going to happen next—reporting back to the full class or making notes for later private work such as extended notes, an essay, short story or film script, helps to give purpose to discussion.

The most manageable initial structure is a series of two or three five- to ten-minute sessions of small group discussion as episodes in a double period, marking stages in the development of a response to a specified text. The well-intentioned but flabby 'Get into groups and discuss the hero here and we'll talk about him later' has little to commend it. Length of time and size of group can grow as pupils mature and as the text demands more consideration. Similarly, the openness of the task assignment can grow as pupils become more complex in their responses and more familiar with a book.

Another approach is that of the 'syndicated group', with each group assigned a different aspect of a text and being made responsible for contributing knowledge about it to the full class. At its simplest, syndicates can summarize two or three chapters of a novel each as a revision aid, but the device can be more open than that. For example, the workhouse episode in *Oliver Twist* where Oliver finally asks for more can be explored in great detail if one syndicate finds out from the novel, and perhaps elsewhere, what conditions were like in the workhouse. Another syndicate can note down all the roles and attitudes of adults in the workhouse, another the actions and dialogue of Oliver, another that of the other children. In the reporting back, each syndicate has a responsibility towards a genuine audience. The other pupils are at least partly informed receivers of what a syndicate is saying and therefore can be more active and perceptive in their comment. This method can be useful at any level, with due patience—and has certainly proved valuable in sixth form studies.

Research into 'teacherless groups' discussing literature has shown that pupils are capable of reaching perceptive conclusions on their own, even if they may *seem* to ramble a little in the process. Pupils should have time to explore on their own terms, as part of developing their response to literature. Excessive teacher control can cause pupils to come to rely on the teacher as agenda maker, rather than devising their own. With due attention paid to how to work constructively, pupils will gain insights into literature—especially if their materials are manageable and enjoyable.

Talk and gaming

There are many games that can be played with a book which involve pupils.

Opposites

This is a handy device since it can be limited to pair work or given to larger groups, depending on the pupils' maturity. Pupils are given a list of opposite features: mature/immature; noisy/quiet; assertive/shy; popular/ unpopular and so on, and are asked to decide which fit a particular character in a novel. Ideally, make the list of features a little inadequate in that it does *not* cover all those you have spotted in the character and in that some of them do not fit him or her. Pupils can sort out which ones to tick, which ones to omit, which ones to amend, which ones to add. More advanced pupils enjoy giving features a numerical rating, '1' meaning that the character possesses that feature to a small extent through to '5' meaning that it is a very strong characteristic. You can also ask for brief quotation or page and line reference, if you wish to have an extended class discussion or later written work. In the early days of using this approach, it is worth keeping work fairly brief—ten minutes or so—and focused on one character. Once pupils have got used to it, syndicates can use the device to look at a character at various significant points in a novel or to look at several characters as they interact.

Interviewing

Pairs can interview one another, adopting roles: a biographer interviewing a character about his or her life in the book; a reporter interviewing one or more characters to build up a story for a newspaper, a magazine profile or *Who's Who*; a policeman or barrister interviewing a villain. The last of these can lead into a full trial scene, calling witnesses for the prosecution and the defence from within the book.

Outside broadcasts

Using a cassette tape recorder, a group can make a 'local radio broadcast' of an event as if it were just happening. 'This is John Leggett of Radio Jura reporting to you direct from Manor Farm. Now tell me, Mr. Jones—you say your animals have just driven you out . . .' This format allows for more characters to be interviewed and can make an interesting group or class assignment, especially if the tape builds in sound effects or music. A few schools have video cameras, making a television news version possible.

'Meanwhile' episodes

Groups can script and tape 'meanwhile' episodes. In a novel, characters go offstage. An account of their adventures and deliberations while they are offstage can provide good material for dialogue or monologue. It also demands knowledge of the text, for the pupils' efforts must be possibilities. For example, in Leon Garfield's *Smith*, the two men in brown must have met to plan how to catch Smith, the sole witness of their act of murder. This would make an excellent opportunity for pairs or small groups to make a dialogue and to present it on tape.

Many of the ideas in the ensuing chapters are to do with pupils' sense of the visual, with drama and with writing. All of them provide further opportunities for harnessing talk.

6

Exploring through drama

The Chinese proverb 'I hear, I forget. I see, I remember. I do, I understand' is a particularly useful starting-point when considering drama as a means of exploring literature and attempting to understand it as fully as possible. A novel is a sophisticated medium with its wide vocabulary, complex syntax, mature (or obscure) concepts, intangible structural techniques, all serving to make literature difficult in some way or other to understand fully. Drama cannot be thought of as an easy solution: it can be a relatively difficult medium to handle in schools for a variety of reasons, not the least being control. The ideas which follow are intended as a means of harnessing *existing* work in drama to explore fiction, and not as an alternative or complete approach.

To give a more precise focus, it is worth considering the use of drama in relation to four aspects of fiction: characterization, setting, inter-action and plot. The description which follows also suggests a sequence which might be followed in building up pupils' confidence and skill in this kind of work.

Characterization

Individual work

'Inside the skin of X' or 'What's it like to be X?' is a sound starting-point. Fiction for young children often uses stereotypes—goodies and baddies, for instance—which help to make the complexities of life more comprehensible. More complex fiction requires a more demanding response from the reader, which this 'inside the skin' technique can assist. Take, for example, *Treasure Island*. Long John Silver has become famous as a stereotype—the school 'comedian' hobbles round on one leg, imaginary parrot on one shoulder, growling 'Ooh, aah'. If handled at a superficial level, drama can promote this stereotyping, but to get inside Long John Silver means talking with the class initially about physical handicap and its effects. 'What must it be like to lose a leg—the phantom pains, the things you can no longer do? What is it like to have to take orders (pupils know all about that)—and from people you know to be less clever than you? What might love of money do to you?'

Drama can be used to explore one text in depth, or several texts can be used to explore a key concept. For example, younger classes can discuss the power which Gollum seeks in J. R. R. Tolkien's *The Hobbit*; older pupils might consider the sorts of power represented by Jack and Roger in William Golding's *Lord of the Flies*. Once the central concepts of either a single text or several related texts have been explored in discussion, individual drama activity can focus upon movements associated with the key characters—ordinary actions as well as the spectacular or highly significant. Some mundane actions might not be described in the book—getting up, dressing, eating—but for pupils trying to get inside the skin of a character, seeing the mundane through unfamiliar eyes is an important stage. The teacher can ask prompting questions: 'How would you hold that object (conch or ring or pistol)? How do you walk when you are angry, or afraid, or in haste? How would you react to a sudden noise behind you?' Questions like these probably have no right or wrong answer. What matters is that they involve pupils as active interpreters of the book. If this sometimes leads to their needing to consult reference books on costume, or to a closer look at illustrations in the text to prove a point, or to their discussing what is unprovable but most likely, then such questions are highly relevant in the process of creating a fuller understanding of the text.

There are conflicting opinions about the 'Everyone stop and look at Julie—she's doing a lovely Long John Silver' approach. Some teachers can avoid its becoming an ordeal or a spotlight for histrionics, but it can have an adverse effect on a lesson's tone. 'Best actor' awards should be as small a part of this kind of exploration of fiction as possible. It is probably more useful to think carefully about holding discussions at stages during the drama work and after it. By this means pupils become involved in verbalizing the insights gained from their improvisation rather than in the techniques of acting before an audience. Discussion during and after the activity should focus on individual impressions of what it was like to be inside the skin of the character. If you see some children moving inappropriately during the activity, for example too quickly and without precision, it is possible at that stage to make them think more carefully about what they are doing. Rather than the 'Don't do it like that—do it like this' approach, it is preferable to ask a question of that child which invites thought. For instance, if exploring the portrayal of old age in R. Westall's *The Machine Gunners*, to ask quietly 'Doesn't it hurt an old man like you to move as quickly as that?' might help the child to concentrate harder. The rest of the class need not hear—it would spoil their concentration if they did, as would more forceful control techniques. The tone used should not be sarcastic. If it is made as a genuine enquiry direct to the child concerned, the response is more likely to be genuine. Then in the class discussion after the activity this issue of speed of movement can be talked over. 'How do old people walk? Why are they stiff-jointed? Is it painful?' If the activity is developed in further lessons, these ideas may have sunk in, being thought about meanwhile by everyone to some degree.

Pairs

Individual work can lead on to work in pairs. One of the pair can be a character explored previously, the other a reporter or biographer—any outsider not in the book—asking about the character's life. An alternative is for the second pupil to take another character in the book, asking the first about an incident during which the enquirer had been off-stage. In both examples the emphasis is on generating dialogue which is not explicitly in the book. The aim is to build up an understanding of the characters and their world, rather than of the text itself at this stage. The process of the drama activity is to look briefly at several characters in this way, the partners changing roles and then reporting to the whole class on difficulties encountered and discoveries made.

Setting

It is probably simplest to consider setting under two categories, at least with younger pupils. One concerns the physical setting of an episode—a room and its furniture, a street, a hillside and, where the author makes them significant, such features as the weather and the time of day or year. The second concerns people as part of the setting in which key characters live and move: the bus queue, a crowd of shoppers, other workers in a factory. They may play no explicit part in the action of the book, but dramatization may bring to light an important feature which the author has chosen to leave implicit.

People and places

After the first stage of pupils on their own exploring character through movement, the second stage is to introduce consideration of the interplay between people and places. Reading to the whole class the most highly atmospheric passages from a text is a good starting-point. Leon Garfield, J. R. R. Tolkien, Charles Dickens, E. M. Forster and D. H. Lawrence are examples of writers who use setting to complement character. After such a reading pupils work through the actions of a character again, but within a particular setting which they try to 'see'. This second run-through is then charged with additional stimulus, and discussion afterwards will aim to encourage their 'seeing', calling on all their senses in describing verbally what it was like, exploring and even expanding on the text.

At a later stage there can be discussion of the more detailed features of the setting such as might be needed for a film or stage version of the book; props, costume design or scenery might be talked about, sketched or even produced. As anyone who has produced the school play knows, inexperienced actors find a few basic props very helpful in establishing character and they should be introduced at an early stage in rehearsal. The same applies to costume. This is usually left until dress-rehearsal, which is a great pity since it takes children some time to become used to its contribution to the complete feel of a character.

It is unlikely that drama of this kind will go so far as full scenery of the stage variety. Certainly there should be discussion of what the class imagine would be the best setting for a play or film version, and this will involve searching the book for clues. *Chapter 7* deals with the sketching of costume, settings and props.

People and people

An important part of the setting is the subtle physical relationship between characters in terms of such items as their relative height, the distance between them or the way they move about within an area. This can be explored in practical drama work. Discussion with the class can concentrate on such issues as, 'Within this episode, who is the dominant character? Would he or she be standing or sitting, and in what way— tense, relaxed, prim, withdrawn? Would he or she move about a lot or not at all? How would other characters move in relation to the main character? Does the mood of the scene change so that another character takes over the dominant role? If so, does that character move nearer to the first? Is this done aggressively?' This can be taken to sophisticated levels on advanced texts. For example, the inappropriate movements of Mr. Elton in making advances towards the heroine in chapter 15 of Jane Austen's *Emma* give scope for melodrama, since his behaviour is grotesque in contrast with the more delicate movements acceptable in Jane Austen's world. For younger pupils Robert Westall's *The Machine Gunners* offers descriptions of a wide range of behaviour from a wide range of characters. A lot more is now known about body language and this can be introduced into the discussion. Most people seem to find the subject interesting in itself. Although such interest may seem to be a side-track as far as the text is concerned, it can heighten interest in the author's skill as stage manager of his characters. Pupils can look at the gestures he has them make, where he lets them move, and at his use of such physical props as their clothes and possessions as means of conveying to his reader comments on their personalities, roles and relationships.

Getting it taped

Another very useful approach to the study of setting, unlikely though it may seem, is through tape-recording. Asking the class to think about how to convey an impression of mood, place and relationships through the medium of a radio play focuses their attention on a particular aspect of the text. Setting is usually established in descriptive passages, which pupils find less interesting than dialogue and action, but translating a passage involving descriptive prose into a radio play with sound effects is an activity most pupils find absorbing. There are professionally produced records of sound effects, but a great deal of the interest lies in home-produced effects. The process of production forces pupils into realizing that setting is a significant feature of the story.

Apart from the more obvious sound effects to set the scene, the presence of a microphone also focuses attention on where the characters are in relation to each other, and what this says about their wider relationship—the confidence which is whispered close to the microphone, the call in the distance, the remark made across a room. Then there is the more subtle area of tone, which tape-recording brings into focus. The author can only give a kind of stage-direction to indicate tone in fiction: '. . . he whispered furtively.' The skilled reader will hear the dialogue of a book in his mind, but the device of a radio play brings some aspects of tone to the fore and can perhaps later promote awareness in the reader when the text is read privately.

Interaction

Having worked on 'inside the skin' explorations of individual characters, and then on characters interacting with setting, the next and much longer stage is the interaction between characters. Most drama and prose fiction concerns interaction, in spite of significant and memorable monologues and soliloquies. From the class management point of view, however, interaction is more demanding than solo work; pupils need to be trained for collaboration. Where there are likely to be control problems, it is advisable to progress from solo work to pairs and then to larger groups, if that kind of division is possible within the framework of the book being examined. For example, in *The Machine Gunners* by Robert Westall, it would be possible for each pupil to work on the character of Chas and such experiences as his finding of the machine gun and the setting up of the dugout, and then go on to explore the characters of other people in the book including the adults, particularly the captured German airman, Rudi. At the interaction stage, pairs of pupils can explore pairs of characters as they interact in the book; for example, the disturbed boy, Nicky, and the girl, Audrey, concentrating on those episodes where she tries to help him. Other pairs might work on the relationship between Chas and Cem, concentrating on the cooperative building of the dugout, or on interactions between Clogger and John. After this stage the pairs move on to combine into fours to explore other scenes in the book, building on the relationships developed by the pairs.

The emphasis throughout these stages is on exploration rather than acting ability. These interactions can be repeated to encourage a deeper understanding of the characters rather than the development of a performance, just as in writing there can be stages of rough notes— outline plan, first draft, final draft—with discussion between each stage on modifications and deletions. Reference back to the book should be encouraged, and if any other groups do watch performances, any comments they make should be of an appreciative and developmental kind: 'I thought that you sounded just like Chas when you said that', or 'You didn't turn away from him; it would look better if you turned away, like the book says.' The kind of questions the teacher asks and the tone of any observations made will influence the kind of atmosphere set up, and should therefore be as supportive and enabling as possible.

As for the dialogue used by pupils in their drama work, it is more important that they establish the feel of a scene than aim for an exact use of the words of the book, at least in the first instance. There is nothing more painful and more likely to kill interest than children stumbling through 'scenes' with copies of the book in their hands trying to read the exact words. It is the spirit of the characters, the pace of the action and the mood of the scene which they are trying to explore. If there are repeated runs through a scene, then perhaps increasing closeness in 'echoing' the text might be one of the aims, but it should not be so much to the fore as to obscure the children's appreciation of *their* exploration of the characters, the setting and the plot.

Plot

The definition of plot as 'a series of actions' is too restricted. Plot is more complex, involving not only action and interaction but also revelation of character and motive, changes of mood and pace, changes of viewpoint. Plots may take many forms. They can be linear, multiple or circular. They can break expectations of the linear through such devices as the flashback, the 'meanwhile' episode, the cliff-hanger and the fore-shadower of events. Given these many facets, with drama's primary focus upon interaction, the medium offers strong possibilities for exploring plot.

Plotting together

Choice of significant episodes for pair or group interaction can lead on quite naturally to a wider consideration of plot. Early on you may have to decide on which episodes are the significant ones to explore, but the developmental process should include pupils taking over the respon-sibility for selection. After work on characters, pupils can scan the book looking for those scenes which involve their character, listing them and deciding which are the most or least important. Putting this information from several pairs together will give a synopsis of the major interactions of the book. Through discussion the class can then identify the climaxes and anti-climaxes, as well as moments in which the dramatic scene is set, a character established or developed a further stage. By sharing such discoveries, the class builds up an impression of the full shape of the book—not just the action.

Writing plays

Once they have identified their choice of significant episodes, pupils may find it useful to draft their episodes as play scripts. The device of a narrator is often used by children. Although it is clumsy dramatically, and would not usually be encouraged in improvised drama, the device of a narrator does help in exploring a text. Not only does it give continuity to a series of scenes, it also physically demonstrates the persona of author, showing how far he or she is present as a describer and how far he or she intervenes as an interpreter or commentator. When later you wish to build up an appreciation of subtle shades of tone in fiction, it is important that children realize that there is a distinction between the views of the author who wrote the book, a narrator whom he or she might have created to recount an episode, and a character in the fiction. Earlier work in drama can help in developing this appreciation.

The developmental process

This chapter has set out to suggest an orderly development of increasingly collaborative group work alongside a coherent investigation of four perspectives (characterization, setting, interaction and plot) which can be used as ways into the novel. Work begins with the exploration of individual characters, moving to individuals trying out these characters taking setting into account. This is followed by interactions between pairs, then groups of characters. The final stage is the building up of a sequence of scenes which represent the significant moments of the book. Such a process is time-consuming but need not be carried out in complete detail with every book. Often the exploration will be much more selective, using only one or two techniques for a particular focus. Nevertheless, as a project which involves much class and group discussion, writing of notes, plot outlines and scripts, detailed reading of a text and precise physical involvement in the meaning of a book, the movement towards a full-scale dramatization of a text has a lot to commend it.

7

Exploring through the visual

It is often said that television's popularity has resulted in children who are far more adept at responding to visual symbols than to the written word. Whatever your view may be, it is certainly worth recognizing that we do rely on what Bruner has called our *iconic* skills as an important means of interpreting the world. The appreciation of literature can be developed and motivation increased if we do promote the constant harnessing of literature and the visual—television, film, cartoon and the pupil's own work as picture-maker, no matter how undeveloped it may be. The first section of this chapter looks at contributions which the teacher can make; the second at possibilities for the pupils.

The teacher

Picturing the scene

Much information to support the setting created by a book or to evoke its vaguer atmosphere can be conveyed by photographs and other illustrations. For instance, Gustave Doré's illustrations of Victorian city life in Blanchard Jerrold's *London: A Pilgrimage* (Dover Books) help with understanding the intense descriptions of low life to be found in *Oliver Twist* and *Bleak House*. Such pictures do not have to fit the text exactly, even when it is a factual background which you are trying to supply. In other instances, it is worth looking at an artist's response to the text itself, for example those by 'Phiz' for *David Copperfield* and the more recent interpretations by Charles Keeping. Quite often a local librarian or a member of the art or history departments can help identify materials quickly and efficiently.

Some teachers find projecting slides or a film strip more effective, the large screen enhancing the image and enabling the whole group to see it. For example, the BBC RadioVision programme *In the Trenches* has been a classic with its skilled, reserved conveying of information and feeling about the First World War. It is a pity that such materials from the Schools Broadcasting service have a limited legal life.

Commercially produced slide and tape-slide programmes are basically of two kinds—*biographical* and *textual*. The former illustrate an author's life, perhaps showing where he or she lived during productive stages of work and scenes which moved the author to write. These can be handy to remind pupils that writers are real people. The other type tries to celebrate the writing itself. This can vary from a close text/picture matching to a freer linking of the text and the visual in which the artist interprets the text, playing a visual game with it. Such devices stimulate some pupils; others may feel that they have had their inner eye dictated to and protest that what they have seen has spoiled *their* version. Any such programme should probably be preceded by work involving the individual's imaginative abilities—some personal jottings, some personal 'writing back' at the text in a form that the pupil chooses, a sharing of anecdotes and so on, so that each pupil has established some degree of *ownership* of the text first—and so that the teacher has some idea of how pupils see the text and respond to it. The programme can then be the focus for critical discussion on the textual–visual correspondence, a sound chance to develop individual critical judgments.

Apart from commercially produced programmes, it is worth considering illustrated talks by visiting speakers. You may need to be cautious about your choice of speaker, checking whether he or she knows the book or topic you are exploring and finding out along the grapevine about the quality of previous talks. A speaker who knew Corfu well and had his experiences and slides to share helped a class to understand something about the partly dated Corfu of Gerald Durrell's *My Family and Other Animals*. A speaker who can give an illustrated talk on life in an early nineteenth-century village or vicarage helps with tackling Jane Austen or the Brontës. If time and cash allow, it is worth compiling your own collection of slides and postcards of a particular author and place (D. H. Lawrence and Nottinghamshire) or of a particular time, for example collecting material on the Romantic period, whenever you come across it.

Magazine articles and cuttings, collections of illustrated books, archive material (increasingly available from some libraries, museum services and famous houses) can all be used for individual or group projects. Alongside such ready-made materials, consider a class making its own tape-slide production. Field trips to Brontë country, Hardy's Dorset or Dickens's London can be followed up by compiling the slides taken on the trip, selecting and sequencing the best and adding a commentary, perhaps including readings from the author's texts. Such a project takes a lot of time, but that can be a virtue, providing space in which to *dwell* with a text and to develop an intelligent and responsive relationship with it. A fine resource book on the relation of writer and place is Margaret Drabble's *A Writer's Britain: Landscape in Literature* (Thames and Hudson, 1979).

The film of the book

Some teachers have long recognized the importance of film as a means of interpreting text. The problem of expense can be partly solved by having several forms see a film together or inviting another school or, if you are in or near a town, getting a cinema to put on a schools' matinée or liaising with its film society. Increasingly films are available as videos, and it may be possible to hire at least one or two videos of books at reasonable rates(**19**).

Films of books are more frequently based on adult fiction than on children's stories and can be a means of helping pupils to tackle more complex fiction as they compare and contrast what the book and the film did or did not do. At the same time, it is worth remembering that for some pupils the visual version is more powerful than the literary. It is probably worth while choosing in the first instance films which are relatively loyal to the original. Where a film does differ, as in the death of the aborigine boy in *Walkabout*, pupils can spend useful time discussing the differences and incorporating their views in their course work. Where the text is set as an end-of-course public examination task, some pupils may have problems over remembering which was the book version unless the literary and visual differences have been summed up and made explicit.

Film in genre study
Fewer schools study literary genres—the western, science fiction, the mystery—but film can be very helpful in such work(**20**). The advantage of genre study is the range of material which can be used, working on clusters of books as a temporary class library rather than studying a single text. Some schools do use a text as a class focus, for example *Shane* for studying the western, Nicholas Fisk's *Space Hostages* for early work on science fiction and Graham Greene's *The Third Man* for senior pupils looking at mystery as a genre. Alongside the book goes a genre box, with its variety of single and small set copies of texts for individual and small group work. Films can be 'the film of the book' but they do not have to be, for the idea is to widen the pupils' experience of the genre, and many good films within a genre do not have a literary equivalent.

Genre study is very much concerned with the matter of techniques, and film is particularly useful in developing an awareness of the match and mismatch between those techniques available to an author and those available to a director. A film can carry several layers of messages—by means of the soundtrack as well as the visual—and can therefore be a very condensed form of narrative.

Through the study of film, younger pupils can be led to see how a plot progresses and how it exploits omissions and highlights; the importance of the setting and the ways in which characters react to it; the creation of a character, starting with the visual components of appearance, manner-isms and movement and going on to the more complex creation through speech and interaction. With older pupils, film can be used to focus on such narrative techniques as the cliff-hanger and the flashback, both visual terms, and the more complicated relationship between setting and mood. Throughout this development there needs to be a cross-referencing of the written and the visual. Film is often criticized for requiring a passive response. In fact, the viewer has to make meaning from it. If its powerful impact is consciously related to an appreciation of literature, both media benefit.

Film and theme

Film can also be used as part of the study of a theme, for example: 'Growing Up', 'The Outsider', 'Living in the City'. This approach to film study is less popular than in the seventies, probably because of the expense involved, but it has much to commend it. In particular, it has a part to play in any public examinations which embody a thematic approach, such as some versions of the Certificate of Extended Education.

Television

Video tapes increasingly replace film, and some catalogues are available of commercially produced videos. Television programmes are often for more immediate use since taping can cause copyright problems and the cost of hiring serializations, where they are available, can be very high. It is often more feasible to use schools' broadcasts, which can be videotaped for a specified period or to use evening and weekend transmissions. The latter can be ideal for some homework assignments, if Head and parents agree. A scheme for noting down ideas needs to be sorted out with the class beforehand. In the case of a serialization, it can grow in complexity as the series develops.

Several recent programmes have set out to promote ways in to a wide range of children's fiction. These are useful as a source of recommendations for buying books for the library, departmental stock or the school book-shop and as a lure into private reading. Class discussions based on such programmes as the BBC's *Book Tower* can be very lively, and it is worth checking the BBC and ITV lists to see what is currently available. The journals *Books for Keeps* and *The School Librarian* give details of forthcoming television and film versions of novels. Exchanging legal tapes of programmes—and of audiotapes as well—can promote links within clusters of schools, cut down on expenditure and provide a chance for teachers to pool their wisdom about the effectiveness of the visual. The basic principles of exploring literature and film or television are not dissimilar, and the study of one medium reinforces and expands under-standing of the other.

Comics

Comics can be useful in two ways. 'Genre' comics—the ordinary funny comic, romance comic, war or sport comic—can be linked with their literary counterparts. Comics extend over a wide age range, from publications intended for very young readers to fully illustrated, extended stories of action or romance for adults. Older pupils might well compare comics for two different age ranges, to see similarities and differences of content and technique and to discuss how their creators view their audiences.

Second, comics often rely on stereotype, cliché and caricature, all devices met more subtly in literature. A structured enquiry in the middle years can look at the topics, characters and characteristics of various comic stories and at the interplay of picture and text. In general, it is worth taking a positive and encouraging stance in harnessing this area of reading, especially since it is often one where the pupils are the bringers of experience and insight.

Pupil activities

Making a context

Pupils can play a great part in creating a setting for a particular text or for a particular theme, for example 'Yesteryear', based on a cluster of such books as Laurie Lee's *Cider with Rosie*, Nina Bawden's *The Peppermint Pig* and Ronald Blythe's *Akenfield*. They can select from the photographs and materials already available within school or from the local library or museum service, if there is one. Better still, they can bring in photographs and objects from home, from grandparents, other relatives and neighbours. This kind of collection is often seen in primary schools, where children have their own classroom and so can build up a collection of pictures, objects, book displays, diagrams, personal writing, art work and other responses without the risk of disturbance by others. Problems of having to shift rooms (and hence of security) and problems of short lessons make it much harder to build up such a display and protect it. Sometimes the library can provide a secure display area. This can come into its own when the library puts on a display of associated books at the same time. In one instance, a display centred on *Carrie's War* contained items as varied as ration books, identity cards, wartime recipes, air raid warden's gear and a child's gas mask, accompanied by further fiction and non-fiction texts from the library's stock.

Exploring through cartoons

Pupils are often asked to make notes on a novel as a means of keeping track of the tale. Sometimes, it is worth encouraging them to think in terms of the visual. Not all children can draw cartoons, but even rudimentary pin-men drawings can illustrate relationships among characters through such items as their relative size, their attitudes towards each other and their intentions, signalled by their actions and gestures. These should be linked to key points of action or of dialogue by means of captions or speech balloons. One pupil, asked to illustrate Leon Garfield's *Smith* as a cartoon strip, chose all the crises—the murder of the old man, Smith's adoption of the magistrate, his enforced 'baptism' when he is scrubbed into civilization—a response which he could not have achieved with his limited writing skills as a first-stage activity.

Exploring through filming

Constant linking of prose fiction to other media helps some pupils to see literature in terms of construct. In making comparisons and connections between a character in a book and an actor's interpretation, between a book's setting and a film's set, between a novel's dialogue and a film's script, pupils are introduced to the distinctiveness of a book and what it can—and cannot—do. The typical methods of theatre, film or television production teams can be used as the stuff of classroom assignments. Some ideas can be very simple:

a) Draw the design for Gollum's ring in Tolkien's *The Hobbit*.

b) Draw the swords of Long John Silver, the Doctor and the Squire in *Treasure Island*. Your designs should be based on the weaponry of the time and the social class and wealth of each man. You should also consider what sort of sword each character would like, with his particular temperament.

c) Sketch the costumes of three characters in *Smith* for the wardrobe department. Explain your choice of design and fabrics. Write brief instructions for the actors/actresses on how they should wear the clothes and how they should move, given their personality and social class.

d) Sketch and make notes on a set you would use for Orwell's *Animal Farm* before and after the revolution. List and explain the features that alter.

e) Sketch the facial features and outline shape of the hero/heroine/ villain of the novel you are studying. Set out notes for the casting director, explaining what kind of person you want to act the part.

f) Draw the plan of movement for the characters in an important scene in the novel you are studying and explain the 'moves'. Include the positioning of any camera and microphones and explain how you want them used and when.

All of these require constant references back to the text. The last one can exploit some of the terminology of the film-maker, not only as a verbal shorthand but also to make pupils conscious of the importance of techniques. It is interesting to see how far authors can be identified as 'filmic' by pupils after they have become familiar with some of the following terms and tactics, here slightly simplified:

Wide Angle	WA	Seeing an extensive section of the scene
Full Frame	FF	The whole body
Half Frame	HF	Half body, e.g. waist upwards
Close Up	CU	Face/hand/ring, etc.
Zoom In/ Out	ZI/O	Moving from far away to close up/moving from close up to wider angle shot
Pan	P	Sweeping across a landscape or setting in an arc from a fixed point
Track	T	Moving alongside a moving object, parallel to it

In most instances, such visualization is best used to look at fairly brief but significant moments in a text. Two simple approaches are available. Pupils can pencil their abbreviated instructions alongside a piece of text and discuss their choices and interpretations. They can also line a sheet into a set of 'boxes' and work within these, producing rough sketches in the first column, referring to the text in the second and making their director's comments in the third.

In Golding's *Lord of the Flies*, for example, this approach is useful in bringing out the change in viewpoint towards the death of Simon in Chapter 9. After the frantic horror of the killing, Golding zooms slowly in so that we are aware of the busy ministry of the sea and its minute creatures as Simon's body undergoes a sea-change. Then he slowly moves out to a wide angle in which Simon's body is seen as part of the universe and of a larger pattern.

Exploring through diagrams and charts

Books which have a multiplicity of characters or a complex of plots can cause confusion in the minds of pupils of all ages, especially when a book is being picked up and put down over a long period, no matter how intensive the study of it is.

In the case of characters, diagrams of family trees can be one way of coping. Pupils can quickly refer to their compilation to see who is related to whom, what relative ages are, what nicknames are used and, through brief comments, what their relationships are and how they change. If syndicates draw up these diagrams and report back to the full class, everyone is involved in work on one aspect of the book's structure from the start.

Such an approach can be extended to all the character relationships— who is the central character (best put at the centre of the diagram), which ones are peripheral, who is sympathetic or unsympathetic to whom (signalled by wavy or jagged lines between them). Further sophistications

FILM TAKE: _Jane Eyre_ Ch. 20. Visit to the Stabbed man

SKETCH	EVENT/LINE REFERENCES	INSTRUCTIONS
	'He turned the key and opened the door...'	FF of Mr. R opening door – Camera to follow him as he goes in with **CU** of his back and head.
	'I saw a room... the tapestry was now looped up and there was a door apparent which had been concealed.'	Pan round room – Z1 to tapestry – ZO to floor and follow the band of light to the open door.
	'A light shone out of the room within...'	Z1 to door's base – tilt up and ZO until full door seen with its bolts – Pan right to the light and go out of focus.

are possible, with each group taking one character and seeing the relation-ships in the novel from that person's point of view. As a class grows in working in this way, further devices can be used—dots and unbroken lines, thin and thick lines to indicate the strength of relationships, for example. Colour can suggest their intensity. For instance, in Jane Austen's *Pride and Prejudice* Elizabeth and Darcy start in chill hostility (blue) and their contact is intermittent (dotted). Later it becomes warmer (perhaps a seemly shade of pink) and more frequent (unbroken line). Such diagrams have been known to produce heated discussion at senior level—and constant return to the book for support.

Where a plot involves a great deal of journeying, as in Anna Holm's *I am David* or Ian Serraillier's *The Silver Sword*, pupils can compile a map. This can be geographically accurate where appropriate, or a map of their own making, creating the island for Theodore Taylor's *The Cay* or the journey in the Australian desert in James Vance Marshall's *Walkabout*. A different device is the indication of the various locations by a series of circles, with the names of characters and brief descriptions of events, actions and relationships written in each 'place'. This method focuses attention on the plot itself, helping pupils to remember the book's outline and to see how the book exploits the travels of its characters. These approaches can start with simple novels, such as Nicholas Fisk's *The High Way Home*. If pupils are trained to appreciate plot in visual terms, they will be able to cope with more advanced stages through to the sixth formers encountering such novels as *Bleak House* with its more complex patterns of physical move-ment and its sub-plots and their various relationships with the main action.

Some teachers find such approaches 'gimmicky', but the visual is a way into a text for some pupils and helps them to see texts anew as they search with particular purposes in mind. Such work can involve paired and group study and reporting orally and visually to others, and its experi-mental use can be justified.

Exploring through book jackets

Designing book jackets is a common assignment and a sound one. Any pupil can have a go, whatever their artistic and linguistic skills, especially if they have considered real covers and their relationship to the text. Some publishers will provide examples of new covers. The layout should be as realistic as possible, based on a sheet of paper of the same size as an actual book jacket and echoing its five section layout, although younger pupils may find tackling the book's front cover enough of a task. The front inside cover should follow the general practice of providing some sort of summary, perhaps an excerpt from an exciting moment in the book and perhaps, details of other books by the author. The front cover itself provides the chance to illustrate the theme as the pupil sees it, with title and author worked into the design. Some pupils may want to carry the design across the spine and the back cover. Others may want the spine to be a separate feature, with the back cover being used for reviews of other books by the author, derived from reviews they have read or, better still, from the views of readers in the school. The back inside cover often includes details of the author and his or her background. Overall, the assignment gives an individual or small syndicate a chance to *interpret* a book, even down to the choice of lettering—quivery writing for a ghost story, computer style for Aldous Huxley's *Brave New World*, and so on. The focus on the visual reduces the amount of writing to be done, in the case of younger and less able pupils; a focus on the written aspects of a book jacket lays stress on succinct and perceptive summary. It is sometimes surprising how much teaching is needed with some pupils, to get them to see how much information a book jacket has to convey—and interesting to see how much detailed reading and revisitation of the text and intense selection, criticism and justification can go on in explaining the design, the choice of items for summary, and so on. In sum, such work demands much more text-related discussion than may initially appear. Wherever possible, the jackets should be used. They can replace, at least for a while, jackets on books. They can also be an excellent means of bringing some of those 'golden oldies' back into circulation—good books which have lost their jackets and which, with 'new' jackets and special display, find themselves being read again. Ideally, such work should have bridges with work in art, as should the next activity.

Exploring through publicity

As an extension of work on book jackets, posters designed by pupils to promote a particular book, a genre or theme, can be very effective. Again, the emphasis is on the link between the visual and the literary—the language of the book and the visual interpretation likely to affect a real audience. Such posters can be displayed in the library or, better still, across the school. Some run advertising campaigns promoting not only particular themes but visits by authors, linking the visit to books by the writer. One duplicates all its posters on A4 paper, so that a copy can be displayed in every form room, advertising 'good reads' for a winter evening, 'lazy reads' for the summer holiday, 'just in' news about new stock and so on, with pupils providing the summaries in the excited language of advertising.

Some schools produce pamphlets of books for particular age ranges, such as newcomers to a school, or on particular genres or themes, again using pupils as artists for the front and back covers.

Another device is for pupils to produce bookmarks on coloured card, to be placed in books in the school or class libraries. A bookmark can be placed in a book to recommend another by that author or another on the

5

Fantasy

same theme or in the same genre or, simply, to recommend something completely different. Younger pupils' efforts tend to be colourful but simple; older pupils may well use some of the features of a book jacket, in a more succinct form. 'What happened when a bully got what was coming to him—and the bully was a farmer? How did his animals manage? Were the sheep really sheepish and the pigs really piggish? Read about courage and treachery, dream and reality in George Orwell's *Animal Farm*.' In all such work, pupils should be encouraged to know books in order to collaborate in selling them to others—in their own form, to younger pupils, to others in the school and, where possible, beyond.

8

Exploring through writing

Pupils spend a lot of their time in school writing. When it is related to literature, writing is often of a 'practical criticism' kind, expecting a response in cool, measured language supported by evidence from the text. It is not surprising that this kind of assignment takes up a lot of time in English work, particularly with senior forms sitting public examinations, although some boards accept work which shows more evidence of the feeling comprehension which this book advocates. 'Practical criticism' is usually a late stage activity, involving maturity and a trained intellect. Its successful development comes about where it is *part* of a wider involvement. A pupil should not only be a critical observer but an active participant in reading a book, using a wide range of abilities of which the intellect is but one. Pushing for immature detachment recalls Dr. Johnson's dictum that 'endeavouring to make children prematurely wise is useless labour'.

Free response

Springboards

Free response writing has a long and honourable history. In recent years, there have been some particularly fine games played back at texts, such as Tom Stoppard's using Shakespeare's *Hamlet* as his springboard for *Rosencrantz and Guildenstern are Dead*, Jean Rhys telling the story of the first Mrs. Rochester, the mad wife in Charlotte Brontë's *Jane Eyre*, in her novel *The Wide Sargasso Sea*, and Auden's poems in response to Shakespeare's *The Tempest*.

Pupils should certainly be encouraged to regard what they read as springboards for their own responsive writing, for in so doing they are likely to sift out features and issues which strike them and with which they might like to stay for a while. They may also echo features of the author's techniques in their own writing—an unconscious assimilation of authorial skills. Some schools set aside an occasional lesson or homework in which pupils are expected to write on from something they have encountered in their reading. This can range from a naïve retelling to a polished and sophisticated extension from the text. Choice of springboard and technique is the writer's. The only commitment is for the writers—pupils *and* teacher—to write.

This sort of assignment can be valuable, provided that writers see it as their chance to make choices. Some pupils find the opportunity a burden and prefer to be given a specific task in the early days, working towards making their own decision as they grow in confidence. Some possible assignments are outlined later under *Focused writing*.

Personal logs

Individual response is important to teacher and pupil alike, whether the pupil is in the reception year or facing the public examination system. Reading a story inevitably involves its remaking within the individual mind, a process which calls upon the reader's abilities and emotions and his or her own life story, including experience of other anecdotes and tales. The process of weaving webs of significance is a complex one, often involving matters which may at first seem relatively small—checking up on the facts of the fiction, such as the names, relationships and attitudes of the characters; checking the values of characters against the values of the reader or of people close to him or her; savouring moments of particular importance to the individual. Sometimes these take place in silence and privacy. Often they follow our usual pattern of coping with the new, the interesting, the puzzling—through shared talk. To devalue the role of such 'gossip' can be a mistake, for it can push pupils into the detached 'law court game' approach of some public examinations far too early and suggest that their natural exploratory responses to a story are not relevant. They need a climate of encouragement over a long period in which to develop not only the social confidence to respond but, deeper than that, the patience and ability to reflect upon their reading.

The keeping of a opersonal log is one means of providing insight into this response to fiction, whether it is fiction by published authors or by the pupil as author in the making. Personal logs help some pupils at least to see that all writers, including themselves, have problems and opportunities in their work as they provide for their readers.

The ideal personal log is a small notebook. One school chops up cheap exercise books into three, so that pupils have a pocket-size log which they can carry around with them—the pages numbered so that it does not become a source of paper for other purposes! Pupils are encouraged to jot down informally personal reactions to their reading and writing of fiction as they go along. Written 'little and often', such notes help to build up a habit which, ideally, should not be seen as a chore. Some forms may need a couple of ten-minute slots a week set aside in which to jot things down, perhaps at the end of a literature lesson or during a library period. Others may be motivated enough to keep their logs in their own time. A log can relate to one text, running a commentary on reactions and details as the reading progresses; it can be a record of personal reading outside the syllabus; it can be a commentary on problems and experiences the pupil has had in his own writing of fiction; it can include comment on fiction in other media.

The log can be part of an assessment system read by the teacher, but if it is to be a genuinely personal document, its owner should have rights of privacy over its immediate contents. Some pupils find the log useful as a means of externalizing how they feel and think; some find it easier to 'talk' to their teacher by handing in their log from time to time for her or him to read and jot down a couple of 'talking back' comments, rather than having to engage in conversation. The log can be the basis of information which the pupil turns to in group discussion, a device found useful up to and including sixth form work. It can also be a means of reflecting on progress, with the pupil writing an end-of-book or end-of-term review on how reader and reading have got on together.

Such work takes patience and tact to develop. Where it succeeds, readers come to see something of the growth of their skills and awareness and something of the complex of abilities they call upon.

Focused writing—characterization

Practical criticism tends to keep some readers outside a text, especially where there is a priority in extracting and analysing features to do with technique. What are also needed are means of drawing a reader into a text. Free response writing is one means of promoting this engagement. Focused writing can be another, developing awareness of authorial techniques by trying them out rather than through analytical discussion alone.

The dossier
The key concept to be grasped is that the author chooses to include—and therefore to omit—certain features of a character, so that he can get the reader to pay attention to significant features. It may be true that senior pupils can quickly produce lists of which features an author has chosen to use in generating a character, but younger pupils may need a more structured approach. One device is to have each reader or small group *adopt* a character—someone from their own heads or from a picture or story. They then have to produce the dossier for that person. Name, address, age, sex, marital status, are easy. Categories such as personality; habits; manner and mannerisms; likes and dislikes; roles; other features, prove more demanding. Dossiers can be used in various ways. One is for another pupil or group to take over a dossier, creating one pleasant and one unpleasant character from the data and then discussing which features they adopted, adapted or rejected in order to create their Jekylls

and Hydes. Another is to circulate or display dossiers so that groups can work out which characters are sympathetic or otherwise and then use their choices for the starts of stories in which characters get on well or do not. Again, the writers should discuss and jot down what they chose to use and how they chose to use it. Senior pupils can examine how far their characterization was explicit, with authorial advice to the reader, or how far it was implicit and how it was achieved—by action, interaction, dialogue, internal monologue, and so on.

'Thoughts in the head of'

This device explores a character by going inside his or her mind. In the case of an existing book, a pupil can write a character's 'inner monologue' at a critical moment in the book when the author has kept outside the character. This can range from setting out the thoughts of the aborigine boy when he meets the white children in James Vance Marshall's *Walkabout* to the thoughts of Frank Churchill as he playfully vies with the heroine at Box Hill in Jane Austen's *Emma*.

Encounters

'When I was with X' or 'When I met X' gives a pupil a chance to imagine himself in one of two contexts. In the first, he can engage with a character beyond the book—for instance, he may meet the white children after *Walkabout* has ended and, assuming that they do get back to white civilization, write of their encounter. In the second, he may enter the book, becoming a character and interacting with others, for example as one of the unidentified choirboys in *Lord of the Flies*. Both provide chances to write dialogue as one means of gaining insight into how characters and relationships can be created and grow in a novel.

Points of view

This is an extension of 'When I was with X'. An author can call upon a range of devices to create character—actions, speech, inner thoughts, others' comments and reactions—and this approach calls upon pupils to discuss which they have used. An episode in a novel is assigned to various syndicates in the class, each group adopting a character who is in the episode or affected by it. The siege in *Treasure Island* can be described through the eyes of Long John Silver, Jim Hawkins, the Doctor, Squire Trelawney and so on. Some teachers find this a useful device when handling a text containing multi-cultural issues, for example the attack on the Pakistani children at the start of Jan Needle's *My Mate Shofiq* can be seen through their eyes, helping to gain some idea of their feelings and of some of the issues the book tackles. The resulting mini-yarns can be used for a class 'read in' and comment on which devices were used to create the various kinds of characters.

Projection
Projection uses information in a book to consider a character in a situation beyond the text. Writing a report as a Welfare Officer on Rocky O'Rourke in S. Sherry's *A Pair of Jesus Boots* involves a knowledge of the text and a response to the characters and their circumstances. So would writing the summing-up speech of the defence and prosecution counsels at Magwitch's trial in Dickens's *Great Expectations*. So would the official report of the rescuing officer in Golding's *Lord of the Flies* as he writes of the tattered, smoke-stained children he found on the island.

Focused writing—setting

A novel's setting causes problems for many pupils, especially where the author spends a lot of his and the reader's time on it. It has its importance, whether it is as passive background or, as in the novels of D. H. Lawrence or Dickens, it has its own life and affects characters and events powerfully. Setting can be seen in terms of place, natural or man-made; time, for example evening or autumn or the Middle Ages; weather; the people among whom a character is placed; the culture in which he or she finds him- or herself. Often the setting promotes an atmosphere or mood, sometimes reinforcing it, sometimes contrasting with it.

Into action
Most pupils like a rapid pace to the plot of their stories and give little attention and reaction to setting. To encourage closer attention to description, pupils can try creating incidents which have a great deal of action in a defined setting but little plot movement—a fight in a western saloon, with blow-by-blow detail; a crisis in a needle match of football; riding a tricksy horse in a high wind; jostling for the star bargain in the first five minutes of a sale. The emphasis is on the eye for detail, with the minimal narrative helping to support the writer who might flounder if there was no sense of time sequence at all.

Camera lens
Descriptive paragraphs of the traditional kind, where the writer has no narrative to help order the detail being described, can be helped by this approach. Because of their familiarity with television and film, many pupils can grasp the techniques of describing scenes and people in camera terms. Younger pupils can cope with *three distance* description, starting with people in long distance, then middle distance and then in close detail, as the characters move in their setting towards the reader or the reader is taken towards them. They can describe a setting from a landing helicopter or a rocket going into orbit. Older pupils might wish to use some of the more detailed techniques outlined in *Chapter 7*.

Quite young pupils enjoy watching a bravura writer create a setting—

the railway cutting in Dickens's ghost story *The Signal Man,* for instance, or the stinking alleys of Tom All Alone's in his *Bleak House* or in Leon Garfield's *John Diamond*. After discussing how a setting might be filmed, they can go on to write their own. They are likely to start with the dramatic and gloomy. Describing more relaxed or more subtle setting takes maturity. Another device is to work from the macro or micro viewpoint, as in Swift's *Gulliver's Travels* in which the hero finds himself in lands peopled by manikins or giants. F. P. Heide's modern text *The Shrinking of Treehorn* can be a useful book here, with the world seen through the eyes of an increasingly small boy. Such writing helps to see items afresh and sometimes in different detail.

Setting the scene

George Bernard Shaw wrote very detailed setting notes for the scenes of his plays. Using these as an example, pupils can work out setting notes for a key episode in a novel. Some texts may well be explicit about a setting; some will leave room for informed conjecture. Younger pupils may find it useful to develop their setting notes from preliminary drawings. Older ones can use reference books or visits to enhance detail or capture atmosphere. In one instance, a visit to a stately home of the relevant period helped students to understand something of the 'superior' world which Elizabeth encounters in Jane Austen's *Pride and Prejudice*.

Responses

Characters in novels may react very differently to the same setting. In Betsy Byars's *The Midnight Fox*, Tommy initially finds the country extremely boring, while his cousin leaves signs throughout the house and the novel of his love for it. Pupils can make notes on these different reactions, perhaps writing contrasting 'day in the life' accounts or an imagined episode where the two boys meet. The responses to the urban tyranny in Orwell's *1984* of Winston Smith, of his interrogator, O'Brien, and of the proles are different and complex, can lead to similar comparative note-taking and could lead to further responsive writing. Characters' reactions to settings can be written as diary entries, as letters home to friends, or whatever strikes the reader. They provide a chance to re-narrate, to summarize and to express obliquely the reader's understanding of a character's personality within a setting and his or her response to it. Younger pupils might write the sort of letter that one of the children might have written in Nicholas Fisk's *High Way Home*, before their desperate attempt to escape from the doomed island. Senior pupils might understand much about Lady Dedlock in Dickens's *Bleak House* by writing at least some of her diary entries, for example during her dreary stay in Lincolnshire at the time of the floods. A C.S.E. class reading Solzhenitsyn's *One Day in the Life of Ivan Denisovitch* was asked to work out how to provide advice to new inmates on how to survive in the labour camp without running the risk of being identified. Their bleak and brief lists on staying alive and how to avoid risks appeared scrawled on cheap toilet paper, on old scraps of wrapping paper, even scratched on a flat stone.

On the inside looking out
Inner monologue has already been discussed as one means of creating characterization. It can also help older pupils to see the interplay between character and place, since the result can be strongly impressionistic, especially if it uses the first person, present tense. A classic example is the opening of Joyce Cary's *The Horse's Mouth*. This is a difficult technique to sustain in an extended story. Careful crafting is often needed if the effort is to be regarded as work 'going public', but it has its place in developing insights into the range of techniques available to an author. Some pupils find the task easier when they are exploring not only a place but a time of day or a type of weather, for example an old street with a fading winter sun, and where they can bear in mind a very defined mood on the part of their character.

Poetry
While it is not a technique to do with writing novels, writing a poem can be one way of evoking a setting. Many poets have done so. Some pupils find that reworking a setting from a novel into a poem of their own making helps them to 'own' it more fully, affectively as well as intellectually.

Focused writing—structure

Many pupils find it hard to realize that a novel's structure is often more than a simple, time-sequenced narrative. The next chapter sets out some of the ways of promoting discussion of the richness which structural choices provide. Some devices are best understood by trying them out.

Plot outlines
Some pupils are so involved with a book's detail that they find it difficult to grasp its overall structure, especially when the book is being read over a number of weeks instead of being block read in, say, a week. At an early stage, pupils tend to find their plot as they go along, but they can benefit from sometimes trying to map out the possible general design for their own efforts beforehand. Some schools encourage younger pupils to write a 'long novel', taking up as much space as they like over several weeks. This can involve an initial note-making phase in which character profiles are compiled and an outline diagram of the book's major events is devised. Comparing their original 'maps' with what they have written shows pupils something about how far an author's intentions are realized or affected during the writing.

Plot variations

The linear plot is the basic structure of narrative, but older pupils can try other devices. Using stereotypes, they can play with such ideas as the cliff-hanger and the foreshadowing of crisis so much used by Charles Dickens and soap operas. The flashback is more sophisticated, but most pupils are familiar with it on film and television and can find it interesting to work out how a novel can use the device. Particularly sophisticated are plots where the same event is seen through several different characters' eyes—a chance for writers to adopt a character each and tell their tale and then discuss their treatment of the device as they pool their narratives. While it may seem one of the more obvious devices to a reader, writing a sub-plot causes many problems. It is often worth letting pupils have a brief attempt at writing with these devices, especially with senior pupils, so that they have time to consider their own efforts alongside those of established authors.

Change round

Quite often the plot of a story is affected by the personality of a character or by some aspect of its setting. Rewriting an episode to obtain a different result by changing one of these can help to illustrate this. For instance, in Golding's *Lord of the Flies*, Ralph and Jack have some initial regard for each other. Rewriting an episode in which that friendship remains strong and hence affects the action can help to show how, in the novel, their relationship worsened and affected its subsequent events. Some pupils have found it interesting to rework episodes with girls on the island instead of boys. The less reverent have removed the characters from their idyllic setting to a polar island!

Off the set

This device, already used to explore characterization, can be used to consider plot potential. Pupils are asked to write what is going on with characters offstage during an episode. Younger ones may want to concentrate on dialogue; older ones can try their hand at the offstage setting as well. This work involves knowing preceding and succeeding chapters, in order to make the offstage episode fit the tale. In sum, the pupils are creating a sub-plot episode which can lead to interesting discussion about what they wrote, what information they used and what techniques they found effective.

Focused writing—style

Style is probably the most nebulous of features to explain. Certainly, direct work on it requires patience and often should be seen as a late stage activity. Contrastive reading and many of the activities already suggested should have helped some pupils to catch awareness of how one author is different from another in his choice of approaches and techniques.

I or he or she?

Pupils can write two versions of the opening paragraphs of a story, using the first person and then the third. The first gives a sense of involvement and immediacy; it also presents problems ranging from how to tackle tenses to how to carry essential information to the reader. The third person provides room for authorial commentary; it may lack immediacy. Younger pupils may not be able to say much beyond which technique they found the more natural to them; older pupils should be able to start to comment on the problems and opportunities each stance provided.

Author, narrator or protagonist?

The distinction between the viewpoints of the author, the narrator and the protagonist can be subtle and important, for example in understanding the ironies of Jane Austen's work. Author-narrator distinction can be demonstrated by getting pupils to create a character very unlike themselves—of the opposite sex, old, criminal, for example—and then have them write an episode seen through the eyes of that character in which they meet and interact for some reason, using dialogue and expressing views. In many novels, either the author or the protagonist narrates the tale. In some, matters are more complicated. Charlotte Brontë has her heroine narrate much of *Jane Eyre* but she herself is narrator-cum-commentator in several places. Jack Schaeffer creates the boy Bob Starrett as the half-aware narrator of his hero Shane's coming into his family's life, in the novel of that name. Conrad also tells some of his tales and sees characters through the narration of another, as in *Lord Jim*.

This aspect of writing can be followed up as pupils try writing a brief passage about an event with the omniscience of the author, through a character created by the author telling of another's involvement and finally through that person's own telling of the tale. Explicit and implicit comment can be developed through fairly simple devices, with pupils writing a brief, directly critical account of a character or event, trying sarcasm and, finally, employing irony.

Sadder, funnier

Young writers take readily to extremes from pathos to farce, perhaps because these produce the most obvious response from their readership. They should be encouraged to do some writing which has a clear idea of what it wants to do to its audience. One device is to outline a 'consequences' event in neutral, telegraphese language—a man walking on the outside of a ladder being knocked down by a cyclist swerving to avoid a warning cone knocked out of place by a falling window-cleaner. Younger pupils can write contrastive versions, one sad, one funny, using whatever techniques they wish. Older ones can widen the range of effects they practise in manipulating an event, producing pathos, nostalgia, anticipation. They can reminisce over an event with regret at its passing and then with distaste that it ever happened; they can anticipate an event with fear and another with eager excitement, using the third person with authorial comment or inner monologue or whatever devices they wish. Throughout, the writing of contrastive passages will help them to see something of how mood and tone have been generated.

Parody

This well-known device can be very sophisticated, but there are many models of its use which can illustrate its techniques without the need for complex, abstract description. Television is one rich source. Parody can be attempted at all levels in the secondary school, but initially the style of the book or passage to be parodied must be obvious. This is where genre study is useful, since the stereotypes of the western, ghost story, romance or thriller can easily lead to gross parodies being written. The more subtle discrimination required to see how writers break out of cliché can only come about once pupils have recognized cliché, a stage which might otherwise come late for some pupils. Parody depends on forms of humour, an aspect which again encourages pupils to think not only of themselves but of their readers and how they wish to affect them. Early results often seem embarrassing and unfunny to an adult, but the benefits in terms of greater awareness of the importance of choosing techniques to do something specific may well repay the teacher's patience.

Pastiche

Encouraging pupils to 'write back' at a text through such devices as 'meanwhile' episodes or seeing events through another character's eyes should cause at least some of them to echo features of an author's style—to engage unawares in pastiche. Pastiche is not parody. With older pupils, trying to write a brief passage on an episode which a particular author might have chosen, using features of his or her techniques and trying to capture his or her attitudes can have particular importance. It can be one way of bringing together the affective and the cognitive, the heart and the head, to find out through conscious imitation features of that author's techniques and, perhaps, something of the effort and achievement of the original writer.

9

Story as artifact

Many of the activities described so far have had as one of their aims that pupils should develop an awareness of how a literary work of art is constructed. Some pupils will go on to make the more formal response of essays and literary criticism which some public examinations expect. This stage requires activities which focus attention on the text and give practice in the conventions of those written forms. The overall approach which this book has suggested so far is still pertinent, promoting active involvement with the text, personal response and enjoyment of the experience. Without these elements, the syllabus is likely to produce only short-term results in pupils who can answer examination questions but who do not willingly read books and who go into adult life as reluctant readers of fiction. The activities described in the rest of this chapter are not necessarily limited to the later stages of education, but they do suggest moves towards the 'law court game' and require analytical skill with, perhaps, the judicious introduction of some literary terminology.

General assignments

The following activities have been used by individuals, by groups or with a full class.

Openings

The beginnings and endings of novels are always important. An effective device to focus attention upon the techniques authors use is to provide the opening paragraph of half a dozen novels and to ask the class to play the Sherlock Holmes Game: *Who* are present? *Where* are they? *When* is the opening set—time of day, year, century? *What* are the characters doing or talking about? *Why* are they there at that time? *What* other significant factors are there?

Pupils make their jottings in two columns, *Stated* and *Implied*, and the answers, reported back, provide a springboard for discussion—initially about the burden of information about character, events and setting, moving on to authorial style and attitude, then on to how far the opening succeeds in luring the reader into the book. Openings which have proved effective include those from Graham Greene's *Brighton Rock*, William Golding's *The Spire*, George Orwell's *Nineteen Eighty-Four* and Keith Waterhouse's *Billy Liar*. Discussion on such a collection of varied openings should be relaxed but brisk, with no passage taking more than a quarter of an hour, otherwise the central points of comparison are lost. Such work should not be assessed if its aims of getting pupils to be honest and to conjecture are to be realized.

The devices open to an author are many. Some stories start with a formula, for instance the fairy tale's 'Once upon a time . . .' which is a safety-net in that what is to be narrated happened not here and not now. Some start with action, some with description of character or place. Some start by trying to evoke a mood. Others switch on the tape-recorder and begin with dialogue. Many use more than one device. By ranging over several openings of novels, pupils can grasp some idea of the variety of techniques available, can categorize them, look for further examples for themselves, and as a later stage, can discuss how one author's use of a device differs from another's without having a sheet of extracts before them. Such sheets of extracts can also be used as 'tasters' to encourage pupils to read further and hence widen their reading beyond the confines of the exam syllabus.

From this kind of work can grow other forms of conjecture. One device is to ask groups to proffer what might be the next paragraph in terms of content and style. Another is to backtrack—providing for them the second, third and fourth paragraphs, and asking them to provide what might have been the first in terms of content and style. In both instances their response might be a fully written-out version, or notes, or an oral account following discussion of possibilities.

Endings

If openings are significant, so are endings. There is the 'back to normal' ending in which all return to their old ways. There is the 'what's happened since' ending which gossips about how characters have fared since the main story ended. Thrillers often have their dénouements, unravelling the complexities of the plot. Some novels have 'unfinished' endings, with their implication that the book's life goes on and that there are more tales to be told. An intense form of this is the 'mid-air' ending where the reader feels bereft, as in Ivan Southall's *To the Wild Sky* which leaves the children stranded with no suggestion of any hope of rescue. Finally, there is the surprise ending.

As with openings, pupils can look across the endings of several novels to see the range of devices used and to discuss their effectiveness. Some teachers may wish to avoid the risk of spoiling the effect of books which pupils have not yet read. An alternative is to give pupils the endings of books they have read and ask them to back-track, seeing how the endings were set up earlier in the text.

Contrast—openings

An extension of the study of openings of novels is to take those which have a similar theme but treat it differently. For example, the openings of James Vance Marshall's *Walkabout* and Paula Fox's *How Many Miles to Babylon?* both zoom in on children who are disoriented and frightened as day dawns, but setting, relationships and atmosphere are powerfully different. Here discussion can extend beyond opening paragraphs to consideration of the full opening chapter.

Contrast—before and after

Since novels usually follow the development of a character through a series of events, plot and characterization are often inter-related in complex ways. Pupils can cope better with complexity if passages which mark significant moments in a character's development are extracted for discussion. A frequent plot pattern is for a character to anticipate an event, to experience it, and then to recall it. Younger pupils may recognize this as the structure of Philippa Pearce's *A Dog So Small*. In Jane Austen's *Persuasion*, Anne Elliot half longs for and half dreads the moment when she will encounter Wentworth, the man she refused in her younger days. The novelist calls on the reader to imagine a younger Anne Elliot, who is only hinted at in the text. The possibility of meeting him becomes an issue in chapter five, is returned to at the end of chapter six, and the anticipation builds up in chapter seven when her brother and sister sing Wentworth's praises. The mood of the heroine shifts a little each time, echoed by the author's style. The event of the meeting itself is encompassed in a single paragraph. The remainder of the chapter concerns Anne's reflections upon its significance. For senior pupils, to extract such passages from the text highlights not only the development of Anne's viewpoint but a major feature of Jane Austen's technique of plot construction in all her novels. This same pattern is to be found in the novels of Thomas Hardy. In *Tess of the D'Urbervilles*, Tess longs for a relationship with Angel Clare, and later spends much time reflecting on it. Jude is fascinated by Arabella in *Jude the Obscure* but their passion turns sour and fades—a marked contrast to their earlier passion.

Another level of before and after is the ageing process—characters grow up or grow old in novels. In *Great Expectations*, the boy Pip grows into a selfish dandy and then into a maturity beyond his years. In Hardy's *Mayor of Casterbridge*, Henchard goes from prosperous maturity to impoverished age and death. Using such texts, students can be given or can search for significant contrasts between early and late representations of a character. A two-column *Early* and *Late* list for points of change and continuity makes the significances clearer and more memorable.

Contrast—authorial revision

It is not obvious to many pupils that the printed text before them has been worked on by a writer who has crossed out words or whole pages, changed the order of events around, altered the portrayal of characters and so on. Looking at two versions of a text can be fascinating for some, if only because they see into the process of writing. More able and mature students, who have the concentration to focus upon detail, can appreciate more fully the preconceptions and techniques of the author concerned. W. Hildick's *Word for Word* (Faber) is a compilation of early and final drafts of extracts from the work of several major writers, and is a very useful source for this kind of close study. The approach has more impact when the work is presented in manuscript form—and museums or art galleries often house manuscripts of famous authors. It has even more impact when a living author actually presents sections of his or her revisions and talks the audience through the writing process. It is certainly worth finding out whether there is an author in your area who will help a class to see how the process of composition works—and whether the author can be booked under your Regional Arts Association 'Writers in Schools' Scheme **(8)**.

Contrasts across texts

Comparing two poems on a common topic has been used for many years as a means of helping pupils to see points of similarity and dissimilarity of content and of treatment. The same device can be used in introducing pupils to aspects of prose. It is sometimes possible to find almost parallel topics. One example is Ursula's terrifying encounter with the horses at the end of D. H. Lawrence's *The Rainbow*, an episode which links well with the short story 'The Rain Horse' in Ted Hughes's *Wodwo*. The school flogging in James Joyce's *Portrait of the Artist as a Young Man* (pp 48–53 in the Penguin edition) has a very close counterpart in chapter 18 of Sean O'Casey's fictionalized autobiography *I Knock at the Door*, with the exception that, in the last, it is the pupil who beats the master!

Occasionally a novelist may have worked the same material in another medium. In the early part of chapter four of *Sons and Lovers*, D. H. Lawrence describes the children lying upstairs as the west wind roars and their parents quarrel. In his very first volume of poems he wrote of the same episode in 'Discord in Childhood'. Comparison of what each literary medium enabled him to do can help some students to see something of the distinctive devices available and their effect.

Finally, two strongly contrasting treatments of a similar experience can be exploited. For example the incantatory, almost surrealist evocation of early childhood at the start of Laurie Lee's *Cider with Rosie* can be compared with the flatly certain interpretation of the world which Michael Baldwin had in his childhood, at the opening of *Grandad with Snails*—and both can be compared with the impressionistic description of infancy in the opening pages of James Joyce's *Portrait of the Artist as a Young Man*.

Syndicates

Collaborative learning is a powerful tool if pupils are carefully trained to work in groups. All can contribute to understanding the text while defending, modifying and clarifying their own responses. Listening to group discussions gives the teacher insight into how pupils 'process' their reading. Sometimes this will justify providing further guidance; sometimes the pupils may well guide the teacher because of their perceptions.

The following assignments lead themselves to advanced collaboration—syndicate work. Here each group assumes responsibility for an aspect of an integrated topic. Each group has the task of reporting back to the others, orally or in written form, so that the separate enquiries contribute to a total picture of the book. Each group, as it reports, is a teaching group. The others, with their knowledge of other, related aspects of the text, are likely to be critical and informed learners. The device has worked particularly well with 'O' level and 'A' level revision classes, the groups looking at such topics as particular characters, critical episodes or significant settings.

Summary

Each group writes a note-form summary of a different section of a novel, listing:

1) characters involved, their relationships and any developments that occur in the section
2) the sequence of the plot or plots
3) the significance of setting.

Requiring more sophistication are notes on 4) imagery; 5) style and 6) the development of particular themes. Groups need to work to a standard pattern of layout so that all the contributions fit together to make one summary, for display on the wall or photocopying. One school produces a pro forma 'dossier' for character reports. Groups should report briefly to the class while the work is in progress in order to avoid mistakes and to clarify ideas.

Crises

Plot can have a tyrannical hold over pupils' attention when they study a novel, and they need to be trained to distinguish significant from insignificant detail. Studying the crises in a novel is a particularly useful approach to understanding its structure since it focuses attention on the larger-scale movements and significant incidents rather than upon the chronological sequence of detail, which is how the naïve reader perceives plot. As a first stage, groups contributing to plot summary will be given confidence that the overall plot can be brought into perspective. The second stage is to get the class to generate an overview of the major movements by assigning to each group one of the major crises or incidents in the novel. Groups apply to their incident the Sherlock Holmes questions—who, what, when, where, why? They then go on to note the techniques the author employs to heighten tension or other emotions in the reader—dialogue, rapid action, repeated words or phrases, cliff-hangers such as flash-back or chapter endings or 'meanwhile . . .'. When groups report to the class, discussion should relate the significance of these crises to one another in the development of the characters concerned and the themes of the book. Such an approach can be applied across a range of texts, from J. R. R. Tolkien's *The Hobbit*, A. Holm's *I am David* and J. M. Falkner's *Moonfleet* for younger forms, to G. Orwell's *Animal Farm*, H. G. Wells's *The History of Mr. Polly* and C. Brontë's *Jane Eyre* for older forms.

Aspects of character

The study of character within a novel can be syndicated, each group adopting a character and following the same guidelines, such as:
1) Give page numbers for a) when your character is present; b) when your character is thought or talked about by others.
2) Say which are his or her most important appearances.
3) Who is your character associated with on each occasion?
4) Summarizing these, describe the part the character plays in the novel.

Where one character dominates the action of a novel it is reasonable to allocate the task to two or three groups, taking early, middle and final sections for study. Novels involving groups of characters, such as R. Westall's *The Machine Gunners* for younger forms, or W. Golding's *Lord of the Flies* for older, are most suitable for this approach. Where characters hold strongly contrasting views, syndication will draw pupils into the more subtle areas of values and attitudes. J. Lingard's *Across the Barricades* offers powerful contrasts between the lifestyle and values of parents and children, between Catholic and Protestant families, between the liberalism of the retired teacher and the sectarianism of some of the other characters.

At a more advanced stage pupils can be asked to take into consideration the extent to which the author makes the characterization implicit or explicit. Some writers make heavy use of direct comment—'Jake was an ugly villain.' Others do not comment directly, all value judgments being made by the reader in response to the actions and interactions of the novel. A half-way stage is for the writer to stand back and allow another character in the novel to make a 'reliable' character assessment. This may lead groups on to the consideration of dialogue and the extent to which a character's judgments are coloured by such other factors as prejudices, loyalties, altruism or vested interests.

Development of character
In some novels there are marked stages in the development of character in terms of 1) self-estimation; 2) values and attitudes; 3) relationships; 4) social standing and 5) fortunes. Using such categories as the basis for making notes, a character's progress can be plotted by groups adopting one character each. An alternative approach is to assign to each group a critical point in the novel, in order to describe the stage reached by all the characters concerned, making comparisons and contrasts. For younger pupils, J. Needle's *My Mate Shofiq* is a suitable text; at a later stage R. Guy's *The Friends* is very good. Both of these books involve the theme of adapting to a multi-cultural society. G. Orwell's *Animal Farm* and A. Huxley's *Brave New World* are suitable for older pupils.

Dominant features

Groups can be assigned different stylistic features or aspects of technique, to consider the ways an author has chosen to affect the reader. Any author is likely to have particular predilections in his or her choice of when and how to use narrative, description and dialogue. Older pupils may find it interesting to analyse patterns in the author's choice of vocabulary. It is important to avoid becoming a sterile word-hunter or grammarian, but looking at the frequency and sorts of verbs, adverbs and adjectives a writer chooses can sometimes give clues to his or her style, as can a predilection for such devices as short, simple sentences or for elaborate ones, for extended description or for terse dialogue. Pupils can also focus on the author's investment in metaphor and simile, or the avoidance of the figurative. The terse, flat style of Ernest Hemingway, for example, makes a strong contrast with the image-studded, hectic quality of the opening of Laurie Lee's *Cider with Rosie*. This work is likely to lead to a more conscious echoing of style in any pastiche which the pupils are asked to write.

Continuity—image

One of the ways of making plot more than a mere narrative is to weave an image or series of images into it. Such weaving can be very subtle and hard for even an advanced student to recognize. It is therefore worth focusing to begin with on a writer who relies heavily on images. For example, in *Sons and Lovers* D. H. Lawrence uses flower imagery as a means of evoking and exploring relationships between his young hero, Paul Morel, and the women in his life—Mrs. Morel, Miriam and Clara. By choosing some of the episodes in which characters react to flowers, students can 'skip' across the book to find moments of similarity and contrast. Page references used here come from the Penguin edition of the novel.

One group can look at two episodes involving white flowers. The end of chapter one (pp 32–37) shows the violent quarrels of the Morels, and Mrs. Morel's night communion with the lilies and white phlox in her beloved garden. This can be contrasted with Miriam's secretive sharing with Paul of her precious white wild rose in the night wood in chapter seven (pp 196–199) and the sense she generates of trapping him. Another group can compare the episode of Miriam sharing 'her' rosebush with Paul, and the immediately ensuing episode (pp 202–203) in which Mrs. Morel shares the delight of her garden with her son.

Another group can look at the use of red flowers. In chapter five (pp 122–124) Paul is 'launched into life' in the form of a job by his mother. Their celebration takes the form of a quarrel with a waitress in a tea shop, and then a fascination with a florist's red and white stocks and a luxuriant red fuchsia—which they cannot afford. This can be compared with chapter 12, aptly named 'Passion' (pp 372–381), in which Paul is launched into the life of his relationship with Clara. The episode opens with Paul buying her red carnations and closes with a wise woman in a tea cottage proffering Clara red and white dahlias. Little wonder that Mrs. Morel does not approve of Clara!

As a plenary session, the group can focus in chapter nine 'The Defeat of Miriam' (pp 290–293) on the episode in which Miriam, Paul and Clara react very differently to the cowslips in a hidden field, and thus display something of their personalities and their changing relationships, as Paul moves from treating the flowers as Miriam would to the way that Clara prefers.

Lawrence was fascinated by the way his characters reacted to living things, be they flowers or animals. Another group will find it relatively straightforward to look at character and relationship when Miriam shows her fear of animals in the form of farmyard chickens (pp 157–159) and Clara shows her fascination with the stallion (pp 287–289).

Lawrence is by no means the only writer to rely heavily upon imagery, but he is one of the more obvious and accessible, and is therefore useful as an introduction. Hardy uses colour—for example in *Tess of the D'Urbervilles* Tess is seen in terms of red and white, while of the men in her life Alec is seen in terms of red and black and Angel Clare as white. Dickens uses anything his imagination will allow. He uses dwelling places and rooms as images of his characters' personalities, as with Krook's horrifying 'shop' in chapter five of *Bleak House*, the genial Mr. Jarndyce's 'Bleak House' in chapter six and the lawyer Tulkinghorn's labyrinthine, sinister house in chapter ten. He uses the weather as an image of the state of society, as in the opening of chapter one, and in images of Esther, Ada and Richard's escape from London at the start of chapter six into the country, compared with the description of Lady Dedlock trapped in the country in chapter two. This can lead to pupils looking for other instances of *pathetic fallacy*—of the weather echoing the mood of a character—in Dickens and elsewhere. For younger pupils there is Peter Dickinson's *The Weathermonger* and its sequels, or Leon Garfield's use of snow in *Smith*, or Betsy Byars's use of a summer storm at the climax of *The Midnight Fox*.

Authorial voice

Authorial voice is a complex concept, likely to be fully understood only by older pupils. It is perhaps best demonstrated in the early stages by use of contrasting passages which show a range of possible relationships between authors and the worlds they create. These can range from the least intrusive stage directions on how a character speaks and moves, to indications of what a character is thinking, to direct judgments on the morality or significance of an event, and finally to the openly interventionist 'Dear reader . . .' voice of nineteenth-century novelists. More complex again are the ambiguous or ironic voices, where the author's relationship to both character and reader is a challenging one, as in Jane Austen's quiet irony or the more mordant cynicism of Jonathan Swift. An underlying question in this respect is, 'What kind of reader does the author assume?' Does the reader have knowledge which characters do not, or is the reader kept in the dark, even misled? More sophisticated questions which pupils may be led to ask are, 'How do I compare with the author's assumed reader? Do I react to the text in the way the author seems to intend?' Here the pupil is being asked to consider his or her personal reactions to the novel as a second stage activity, having previously studied the techniques of the author.

Such collaborative enterprises as the above take time. They are justified when they provide opportunity for shared reflection in which pupils shape and develop their initial reactions to a text through focused study and become more aware of their own responsibilities and achievements as readers. At its best such work has a part to play in leading pupils to a deeper 'feeling comprehension', which is the central purpose of this book.

10

Towards the good reader

Emerson's comment that 'tis the good reader that makes the good book' has some truth in it if it is taken as meaning that increasing competence and confidence help a reader to enjoy books shrewdly and positively.

Most 'simple' reading likes to move fast, to get straight past the language to the story's people and events. Adults and children alike enjoy such reading, for example the skelter through a fast-moving, action-packed yarn. Sometimes there is another pleasure to be had, gained through reading at a slower pace or even stopping for a while. This is the pleasure gained in appreciating the skill of another human being in producing a work of art and in becoming aware of one's own achievement as reader in sharing with the author an exploration of the human condition. This book has set out to describe some forms of classroom practice which aim to develop awareness of how a novel is formed by writer and reader, without working against the pleasure of 'simple' reading; which believe that enjoyment of a novel can often be increased through a myriad of ways, some private, some actively shared, but all asking for reflection; which hold that 'feeling comprehension' enables at least some readers not only to reflect upon the worlds within books but to gain insights into the world in which they exist.

Our brief has been to look at fiction in school—in its classrooms and its libraries. We have therefore tended to focus on classroom practice and texts encountered in schools. At the same time, we hope that our discussion has shown the width of the concept of 'fiction' in its drawing upon interests in television, film, comics, picture books and anecdote, whether these come from pupils or teachers.

All this demands a shrewd, sympathetic knowledge of adolescents. It also expects an involvement with reading and a wide knowledge of books. Both can take a lot of time. A commitment to reading and to sharing views and ideas with pupils and colleagues helps insights to grow. In *all* of this work, two key notions are crucial to success. The first is *reciprocity*, the readiness to create a climate in which everyone is an equal, including the teacher. The element of mutual inquiry, mutual pleasure, mutual support is essential. The other notion is *involvement*. We should be seen to read when everyone else in the class is reading; we should be seen to write or draw or diagram when others are doing so. The more we are seen to be engaged in the risks and challenges and tasks ourselves, the greater the chance of pupils trusting the process and helping to create the climate in which making personal, responsive, intelligent meaning through encounters with books can grow.

As for the suggestions in this book, we readily acknowledge our debt to the many generous colleagues who have talked to us and worked with us over the years. Some of the ideas may be 'instant successes' for you; some may flop; most will take time to try out and nurture. The best approach to any of them involves 'positive scepticism'—intending to make them work, being realistic about what happens and bearing in mind that you have the professional right to adapt them to fit you, your pupils and the books which you share.

Doubtless you are already aware of further tactics and strategies and will go on to devise many more. We hope that you will share them, for there is much still to be done in understanding how young readers can be helped to delve into fiction and enjoy doing so. The ideal climate is a collaborative, inquiring, supportive one within the classroom itself, in a department, a teachers' group or, at its simplest, talking with someone else who is interested.

The rest of this book provides further examples of classroom practice and the addresses of various support agencies and publishers you might wish to make use of. It also suggests some reading, ranging from current bibliographies of children's fiction to present thinking on adolescents and the reading process. We hope that you find these a useful extension of this book.

References

1 D. W. Harding 'Response to Literature' in M. Meek et al., *The Cool Web*, Bodley Head, 1977.
2 N. Tucker 'How children respond to fiction' in *Children's Literature in Education 9*, November 1972. See his *The Child and the Book* for fuller exploration.
3 See Appendix 6.1.
4 See Appendix 6.3.
5 See Appendix 7.1.
6 See Appendix 6.3.
7 See Appendix 7.2.
8 Your local library should have the address of your Regional Arts Association. Otherwise check with the Arts Council (Appendix 5) or in *Children's Books: an Information Guide* (Appendix 6.1).
9 J. Ingham *Books and Reading Development*, Heinemann Educational Books, 1981.
10 See Appendix 5 for address details.
11 See Appendix 5.
12 See 8.
13 See Appendix 6.1, for example Collins (Fontana Lions) and Puffin.
14 See Appendix 6.2.
15 G. Josipovici 'The Lessons of Modernism' in *The Lessons of Modernism*, Macmillan, 1977.
16 For a different view, see A. Chambers, *Plays for Young People to Read and Perform*, Signal Books, 1983.
17 See the work of D. Barnes in such books as *From Communication to Curriculum*, Penguin Education, 1975.
18 P. Blackie 'Asking Questions' in E. Grugeon and P. Walden, *Literature and Learning*, Ward Lock, 1978.
19 See Appendix 3.3.
20 See Appendix 3.3.

Appendix 1

Preparing a book for the classroom

Some teachers like to 'follow' a book—to think of ideas about how to respond to it in the classroom as they go along. Some believe that discovery favours the well prepared mind and prefer to have spent some time with the book beforehand. Here is an example of working up ideas on Leon Garfield's *Smith*, a book quite often used in the lower forms of secondary schools, based on an approach by Alan Hale.

The teacher has produced a four section *aide-memoire*, which should see pupils through the duration of their work on the book. The first section keeps track of the story. The second suggests any interesting items about the book's language. The third contains any ideas which crossed the mind during reading the book. From these three comes the fourth, a compendium of possible activities. The idea is *not* to use all of them, and certainly not to stop mechanistically at the end of every chapter to 'do some work' on it—but ideas have been jotted down before they can be forgotten, for the benefit of the teacher and for the benefit of any colleagues who want to use the same book.

This effort took just under six hours, spread over a week or so—a leisurely reading of the book simply for pleasure, followed by a skim read and jotting down of ideas as you see them here. That may seem a large expenditure of time, but it can also be seen as a shrewd investment. If a teacher can produce one of these 'dossiers' a term, he or she has three at the end of a year; a department of three teachers would have nine, and so on. If two schools agree to share copies of their dossiers, considerable quantities of books can be covered. The results of such effort outside the classroom can be a reduction of unnecessary effort and an enrichment of work possiblities inside it—and adapting ideas for yourself and your pupils from someone else's dossier often generates new ideas and clarifies them.

Chapter one summary	Language features	Links in and beyond the book
Young London thief, Smith, pickpockets old countryman. Old man who fails to find something wanted by unseen men with a limp. Smith horrified by the murder and frustrated over his pickings, a letter, because he cannot read.	* Idiosyncratic style—energetic/hectic catching the rush of Smith's life. * Uses eighteenth century words for objects, e.g. *carricle* and slang words, e.g. *jug.*	* City book—look at C18 London and its buildings, high or low. * Cf. London of Dickens, e.g. in *Sketches by Boz.* * Petty crime—see pickpocket training in Dickens's *Oliver Twist* and Mayhew on London low life.

Chapter one possible activities

A.   Jot down the thoughts inside Smith's head as he hunts the old man—as he picks his pocket—as he sees the murder—when he sees what he has stolen.

B.   Use some coloured paper, for example blue/brown/grey sugar paper and black and white, for example charcoal and chalk, to sketch the setting of a menacing part of the town. (This can form the background for mounting later work, or you can add notes to it, as if you were sorting out some shots for a film of the book. The illustrations in the book may give you some ideas, but don't copy them exactly.)

C.   Go on a metaphor hunt in the chapter with your teacher.

D.   The author often uses a lot of nouns or a lot of verbs together. Go on a 'cluster hunt' with your teacher.

E.   This chapter uses lots of words from about two hundred years ago. Hunt for them and see if you can find out their meanings.

F.   Act out Smith's hunting, the murder, the rummaging of the body. Write a script first, if that will help.

G.   Turn part of the chapter into a 'radio play' as a group and put it on tape.

H.   Liaise with the art department on C18 architecture of all kinds and with the history department on the period's social life.

Chapter two summary	Language features	Links in and beyond the book
Smith goes home to sisters' basement in an inn, where they live by altering clothing, including that of the hanged. Bridget and Fanny cannot read the letter either. None of them trusts showing it to anyone else.	* First extended dialogue—Smith's cheek towards the landlord. * Pseudo genteel language of the sisters.	* Altering clothes—work on C18 dress. * Living in an inn.

Chapter two possible activities

A.   Continue with items **C** and **E** from the previous chapter.

B.   Miss Bridget and Miss Fanny are seamstresses. Present illustrated mini-lectures on the dress/costumes/uniforms of the time for various levels and occupations. If you can get to the costume section of a local museum or get the needlework department to help, do.

C.   This is a society in which nothing is wasted, not even a dead man's clothes. Compare it with our own.

Chapter three summary	Language features	Links in and beyond the book
Smith pesters people unsuccessfully to teach him to read—Newgate debtors, passers-by, priest, bookseller. Causes bookstock to collapse. 'Someone' finds out from the bookseller who Smith is and where he lives.	* Dialogue between Smith and various people of higher social class—his wheedling politeness and his use of insult.	* Prison—description of prison at end of *Pickwick Papers* and in *Sketches by Boz*. * Desirability of illiteracy—W. Somerset Maugham's ironic short story *The Verger*. * Quest theme—here, the quest to read. Cf. extensive range of books, TV programmes on journeying/searching for something.

Chapter three possible activities

A. Write a brief drama script with Smith and *one* of the people he asked to help him to learn to read, as if they had talked for about two minutes—the lawyer/schoolmaster/elderly lady in the carriage. Don't forget to give your two characters different speech, and don't forget Smith's efforts to be polite as he asks for help and the ease with which he can be very rude when he is refused!

B. Do a chaotic drawing which captures the chaos in the bookshop when all the bookshelves come tumbling down.

C. Continue with items C and E from the first chapter.

D. Smith sets out on a quest—to learn how to read. Share ideas in a 'may we recommend' session about other books people in the class might find interesting where children or adults seek for something. (Examples include A. Holm's *I am David*, J. V. Marshall's *Walkabout*, I. Serraillier's *The Silver Sword*, and so on.)

E. Some of the characters tell Smith he is better off not being able to read and write. What do you think? You can be serious or comic in a discussion on this topic.

F. Listen to your teacher read W. Somerset Maugham's story *The Verger* on the advantage of not being literate.

G. Listen to your teacher read a description of a prison written by a Victorian author, Charles Dickens.

Chapter four summary	Language features	Links in and beyond the book
Smith returns to basement. His hero, highwayman Lord Tom is there, but Smith is uneasy about showing him the document and lies about it. The landlord tells Smith that two men in brown have been looking for him. Terrified, he rushes out.	* Characterization through dialogue—tawdry swagger of Lord Tom, sentimental nature of Fanny, crisp practicality of Bridget. * Description by two men in brown of Smith.	* Highwayman as hero—Dick Turpin, etc. The 'romance' of certain forms of crime. * Cf. Alfred Noyes *The Highwayman* illustrated by Charles Keeping (Oxford 1981).

Chapter four possible activities

A.   With your teacher, begin to look at the starts and ends of chapters, to see the tricks the author is using to try to hold your interest.

B.   Start a chart of who appears in which chapter.

C.   Lord Tom sees himself as something of a hero. Present mini-lectures or contribute to a mini-book of highwaymen, small arms, carriages and road systems in the eighteenth century.

D.   Contribute to a class discussion on who are popular heroes nowadays.

E.   Read *The Highwayman* by Alfred Noyes, illustrated by Charles Keeping for one view of the highwayman. Read *Gentleman Jim* by Raymond Briggs for the story of a man who always wanted to be a highwayman.

Chapter five summary	Language features	Links in and beyond the book
Smith unsuccessfully hunted by the men in brown. Drunk, Smith knocks over blind magistrate, Mansfield. In pity, Smith leads him to his mansion. Smith aware of irony of knave helping man of justice—and irony that neither of them can read.	* Characterization through dialogue—Smith (young knave) and Mansfield (absolute justice but vulnerable). * Author building in his own comments and trying to build in insights into characters' psychology and values.	* Description of low life city—inn and inn signs; streets and street names. * Link with ch. 1—then Smith the hunter, now the hunted. * Smith as Good Samaritan.

Chapter five possible activities

A.   Compare Smith the hunter in chapter 1 with Smith the hunted at the start of this chapter. Write Smith's thoughts as he is tracked through the London streets. Then compare what you have written with what you wrote for the first activity in the first chapter.

B.   The author describes many features of the city during the chase. Do some research on what is old in your town or village, especially the smaller things, such as inn signs, street lighting, bollards, door knockers, and so on. Your art and history departments may be able to help you; so should your local library or museum. Produce a class display in poster form or contribute to a mini-booklet on the topic of 'the old in the new'.

C.   If you have had any success with the previous assignment, produce a drawing as you did for chapter 1, but this time based on your own locality. Then write the opening page of a novel to go with it, making it as gripping as you can.

D.   The author uses lots of street names here. With help from your teacher, do some work on the street names of your locality and where they came from.

Chapter six summary	Language features	Links in and beyond the book
Smith in Mansfield's house—hostile reception by Miss Mansfield which the father cannot see. Smith taken on as servant after a mighty scrubbing. The document disappears from his room.	* Mismatch between Miss Mansfield's spoken language to her father and her real feelings and their display in her body language.	* Smith's great tubbing—hygiene in C18; herbs and their properties; Daniel Defoe's *The Great Plague*. * Miss Mansfield's manner—Garfield's preoccupation with the theme of 'seeming and being'. Cf. Garfield's *Jack Holborn*. Cf. Father, daughter and boy in Garfield's *Drummer Boy*.

Chapter six possible activities

A.   Working in a small group, produce a drama script about an episode where Miss Mansfield is furious with her father about something but does not say so. You will need to include stage and acting directions, so that 'Miss Mansfield' will know how she should act to show her fury to the audience.

B.   Dramatize, with or without a script, Miss Mansfield's poking Smith out from under the bed.

C.   Write as a piece of the novel or as a short scene in a play the preparations by the four footmen as they get ready to trap the smelly brat, Smith, to give him a good tubbing.

D.   Miss Mansfield can seem calm to her father when she is in fact very angry. 'Seeming and being' is a favourite theme of this author. Contribute to a sharing session on books or television programmes where people aren't what they seem to be and what the consequences are.

Chapter seven summary	Language features	Links in and beyond the book
Smith wretched at loss of paper—told by scullerymaid she had replaced it in her master's study, thinking it was his. Smith caught in study by Miss Mansfield but given another chance. Miss Mansfield being courted by a solicitor, Mr. Billing.	* Dickensian imagery, e.g. scullerymaid's arms 'the colour of boiled lobsters'.	* Link with ch. 3—Smith's second avalanche of paper.

Chapter seven possible activities

A.   The author is like Charles Dickens in his liking to be a bit outrageous now and then. Dickens once saw a clergyman's unconscious wife being carried upstairs 'like a grand piano' and Garfield sees the scullerymaid's arms having 'the colour of boiled lobsters'. In pairs, take part in an 'outrageous image' competition. (The only rules are that you mustn't name names and rude rudeness is banned!)

B.   Draw the chaos in the study. Compare your effort with the drawing of the bookshop in chapter 3 that you made.

Chapter eight summary	Language features	Links in and beyond the book
Smith taught to read by Miss Mansfield who becomes fond of him. She keeps him away from Mr. Billing, in case they don't get on. Mr. Billing is shattered when he finally sees Smith and rushes from the house. He returns and claims that Smith murdered the old man.	* Description of alphabet in terms of equipment in Newgate Prison.	* Link with ch. 3—scullerymaid deplores literacy.

Chapter eight possible activities

A.   Design a 'Newgate Alphabet'.

B.   Write two pages of a learning-to-read book **a)** as Miss Mansfield might write it and **b)** as Smith would want it.

C.   Smith learns to read—a great achievement. Describe a moment of achievement in your own life or the life of someone you know, and the steps leading up to it.

D.   The end of the chapter is a trap, with Smith expecting something splendid to happen and then something awful happening instead. Describe an episode in your own life when something unexpected happened, or make one up. Like the author, try to keep the suspense going until the moment of shock.

E.   We are not present when Billing tells Mansfield and Miss Mansfield that Smith is the murderer. Write the scene when he does so as you think the author would have written it, up to the lines Billing says towards the end of the chapter.

Chapter nine summary	Language features	Links in and beyond the book
The Mansfields reluctantly believe Billing that Smith was the murderer. Billing accompanies Smith in the carriage to Newgate—and cajoles and threatens him unsuccessfully to reveal the whereabouts of the document.		* Theme of trust and betrayal of trust.

Chapter nine possible activities

A.   In the previous chapter, the Mansfield servants were very fond of Smith. Now they even spit on him. Write and put on tape the jostling of the hostile servants as Smith is led to the carriage on his way to Newgate. (Don't forget the kindness of Meg, the scullerymaid.)

Chapter ten summary	Language features	Links in and beyond the text
Smith in Newgate. He is visited by his sisters and Lord Tom, and then by Billing, who claims that the chief villain is a 'Mr. Black'. Smith claims to have forgotten where the document is.	* Tyburn Carol at end of the chapter.	* Link with ch. 3—Smith then a visitor to Newgate, now a prisoner.

Chapter ten possible activities

A. Write your own version of the Tyburn Carol, with its bitter and sad overtones—or write a school one!

B. The Stone Hall is a strange place. Decide on appropriate art materials and draw part of it as you think it must have looked.

C. Smith says bitterly, 'I've had enough of trust to last the rest of me life.' Our lives depend on trusting each other—that our doctor does want to cure us, that people will obey the Highway Code, and so on. Make a list of all the people someone has to trust—a train driver, or a teacher or someone going shopping—and why he or she has to trust them.

D. Æsop wrote several fables about trust and treachery. Have a look at some of these and then write one of your own for a class collection.

E. Smith is innocent but helpless in the power of the lying Mr. Billing. Write a story in which someone is in a similar situation.

F. Imagine that Billing keeps a diary. Write the entries he makes for his visits to Smith in this chapter and the next, so that they show what sort of character he is.

Chapter eleven summary	Language features	Links in and beyond the text
Billing continues to visit Smith. Meg the scullerymaid is persuaded by Smith to try to find the document and bring it to him.		* Dreams—dreams in other tales.

Chapter eleven possibilities

A. The old man in the grate is a strange person. We are told he dreams a lot as he lies there. Think of a dream he may have as he drifts in and out of the reality of the prison and then write a passage in which you catch the moments of his dream and its weaving into the reality of the Stone Hall, with its people and noises and movements.

B. The devil strikes bargains with Smith in his dreams. Write the dialogue of Mr. Mulrone the highwayman in his dream with the devil or the dream of Mr. Billing and the devil, trying to use the style of the author.

Chapter twelve summary	**Language features**	**Links in and beyond the book**
Meg disturbed the men in brown in Smith's room and did not get the document. Smith is pleased, since this means that Billing still needs him. He arranges to escape up the ventilation system. Mansfield arrives with the document, Meg having told him of it. He intends to take it to its addressee, Billing's co-solicitor, and ignores Smith's warnings that he will be murdered.	* Evocation of spirit of place at start of chapter—city stilled and blessed by the snow.	* Robert Bridges' poem *London Snow*.

Chapter twelve possible activities

A. The chapter opens with a full and detailed description of the place and the season. Imagine you are at the same scene at the height of a humid summer and describe it as if it were the setting of the chapter.

B. The men in brown are found in Smith's room. Write the dialogue as they get into Mansfield's house, go to the room, ransack it, are discovered by Meg and dash out. If possible, tape the result as a radio drama.

C. Doubtless the men in brown had to report their failure to Mr. Billing. Write the meeting as the author might have written it.

Chapter thirteen summary	**Language features**	**Links in and beyond the book**
Smith clambers up the ventilation labyrinth to the roof but finds the men in brown waiting for him. He slips down a ventilation tunnel into an area of the prison where a crowd is giving a send-off to highwayman Mulrone on his way to Tyburn. Smith escapes under his sister's skirts.	* Description of the trip up the ventilation system—especially the use of sound.	* Ventilation system—chimneysweeps in C18 and C19, in Mayhew, etc. * Claustrophobia. Cf. the cave episode at the end of Mark Twain's *Tom Sawyer* and in Alan Garner's *Weirdstone of Brisingamen*.

Chapter thirteen possibilities

A. Sketch the snow-capped prison roof as the men in brown wait.

B. Write the dialogue of the men in brown as they wait in the cold, hear Smith coming, see him, reach for him—and lose him!

C. Invent a board game—perhaps based on *Snakes and Ladders*—of Smith in the prison trying to get out.

D. Smith is in an extremely enclosed space. Many people are frightened of such situations and are said to suffer from claustrophobia. Look at some episodes in other books where people are trapped. See the cave episode at the end of Mark Twain's *Tom Sawyer* or the cave episode in Alan Garner's *Weirdstone of Brisingamen*.

E. Apart from a curious, brief mention in the final chapter, this is the last one to spend any time with the old man in the fireplace. Backtrack to chapters 10, 11 and 12 and then write a description of him.

Language features	Links in and beyond the book
* Argument between Lord Tom and Miss Bridget about their contrary views on highwaymen.	

Chapter fourteen summary

Back home in the basement, Lord Tom works out when Mansfield will have to cross the notorious Finchley Common to deliver the document, so that he and Smith can waylay him and save him from the men in brown.

Chapter fourteen possible activities

A.   This is the last chapter with any extended description of Smith's sisters, Miss Fanny and Miss Bridget. Working in a group, adopt one of the sisters and backtrack to chapters 2, 4, 10, 11 and 13 to find out all about them. Then build up a description of your character for presentation to one of the groups working on the other sister.

B.   Lord Tom, Miss Fanny and Miss Bridget have various views about crime in general and highwaymen in particular. Imagine them in the basement having a discussion which gets rather heated. Set it down as a script for taping, to last two minutes.

Language features	Links in and beyond the book
* Evocation of snow-bound heath.	* Links with chs. 6 and 9 on the theme of 'seeming and being' and with ch. 10 on the theme of trust. * Cf. the snow-stilled city in ch. 12 with the snow-swept heath.

Chapter fifteen summary

Lord Tom and Smith go to an inn on Finchley Common to await the coach. Lord Tom goes to another inn—and Smith, playing with a spyglass, sees him talking to the men in brown. He sees the coach coming, rushes into the snowstorm, and pulls Mansfield from the coach into a snowdrift, so that Lord Tom and the men in brown find an empty coach.

Chapter fifteen possible activities

A.   Produce a film script for the chase across the heath, up to the pulling of Mansfield from the coach. Fold a sheet of paper in half and draw lines across it. (See the sketch for *Jane Eyre* on page 45.) Put your sketches for each bit of the film in the left-hand side and any instructions about filming, dialogue, sound on the right. (Don't be too fussy about the drawings—pin men will do.) Use the following code to save time: LS = Long Shot; FF = Full Frame (whole body); HF = Half Frame (e.g. upper half of body); CU = Close Up (e.g. detail of face); ZI = Zoom In (e.g. camera focuses in from LS to HF or CU); ZO = Zoom Out (reverse of ZI); P = Pan (camera moves round in an arc to get a panoramic shot; T = Track (camera keeps alongside moving object, e.g. horse racing).

B.   Look at the description of the snowbound city in chapter 12 and the description of the snowbound heath here, and make a list of the differences for a class discussion.

Chapter sixteen summary	Language features	Links in and beyond the book
Smith leads Mansfield in silence, fearing the blind man's absolute justice, but then pities him. Smith and Mansfield are reconciled. They find sanctuary in the heath constable's cottage. Mansfield lies over Smith's identity, to cover for him, and hands the document to Smith—images of trust.	* Dickensian description of Constable Parkins's excessively neat, 'law and order' cottage. * Dickensian caricaturing of Constable Parkins's language.	* Description of caricatured people in Dickens. * Caricatured language, e.g. Mr. Winkle's manner of speaking in *Pickwick Papers*. * Fine example of 'pathetic fallacy', the weather echoing the mood of the characters and their predicament.

Chapter sixteen possible activities

A.   This is the last extended description of the weather—here, a blizzard. Backtrack to other descriptions of the weather, for example in chapter 12. Contribute to a class discussion on how the weather gets used to set the atmosphere in this book and any others you can think of.

B.   The Parkinses' house is excessively tidy. Write a description of an excessively *untidy* house and its occupants.

C.   Your teacher will show you some of Mr. Winkle's nervous, clipped language in *Pickwick Papers*, which you can compare with the excessively tidy, nothing wasted, smug talk of the Parkinses. Now write your own effort at caricatured language for various types of people and various occupations—for example, a gloomy schoolteacher, a fiery bus conductor.

Chapter seventeen summary	Language features	Links in and beyond the book
Smith reads the letter. The old man, a Mr. Field, had been in fear over a terrible discovery. Mansfield and Smith start up to the village old Mr. Field had come from. Mansfield talks of family quarrels, and of how Mr. Field's son disappeared many years before and was probably dead. Smith has an uneasy feeling that they are being followed.	* Use of a character to provide flashback information via dialogue.	

Chapter seventeen possible activities

A.   Read the bits of description about the letter and then re-create it in full, remembering what sort of man it was who wrote it from the brief comments on him in chapter 1.

B.   Smith is uneasy about being followed. The book has used lots of devices to make you feel uneasy. Write a chapter of a novel in which everything *seems* fine, but . . .

Chapter eighteen summary	Language features	Links in and beyond the book
Smith and Mansfield go to Mr. Field's house, which has been torn apart by his sister and nephews as they hunt for his supposed fortune. Smith finds where Field's son used to play (a clue in the letter) and leads Mansfield to the cemetery—where Smith sees a one-legged man waiting for somebody.	* Description of the plundered and bare house. * Contrast in descriptions of the hectic sister and the dourly loyal manservant.	* Plundered house—Cf. Miss Havisham's house in *Great Expectations*. * Cemetery and its gravestones—work on C18 and C19 gravestones and church memorials.

Chapter eighteen possible activities

A.   Here is another place in chaos, torn apart in a search for something. Describe the scene as Mr. Field's relations roam through the house searching for the fortune. You can either tell it as the author would have done or tell it through the character of the old, loyal, embittered servant, Andrews.

B.   Produce the film script of the last page of the novel as Smith drags Mansfield to the climax with the figure sitting on the tombstone.

Chapter nineteen summary	Language features	Links in and beyond the book
Billing arrives and talks to the one-legged man—who is old Mr. Field's long-lost son and also the mysterious 'Mr. Black'. Billing had got 'Mr. Black' to try to block the incriminating letter by murdering Field's servant, but it was Field himself who was killed. The two villains and the men in brown see Smith and Mansfield's footprints in the snow and prepare to kill them. Lord Tom appears and redeems himself by defending them. Lord Tom is killed, a hero, and 'Mr. Black' is tracked and killed by Mr. Field's old servant. His secret was that he was wanted on a capital charge. Billing escapes.	* Use of dialogue as flashback device.	* Dénouements in other novels. * Righteous vengeance in other novels.

Chapter nineteen possible activities

A.   This is the last appearance of Lord Tom. Look at him in chapters 4, 10, 14, 15 (and 20) to build up your knowledge of him. Go to chapter 15 and look at Mr. Bob, the innkeeper, and the way he speaks. Imagine Mr. Bob telling his cronies at Bob's Inn all about his friend, his dashing ways and his heroic end *or* write the story of Lord Tom as a ballad.

B.   Using the weather and the bleak countryside to create atmosphere, describe in detail the old servant, Andrews, as he hunts his loved master's villainous son through the winter snows and finally kills him as an act of avenging justice. You can tell the story as if you were Andrews or the son, or you can write the story as you think the author would have told it.

C.   Billing disappears for a while. Write about his life on the run.

D.   Billing is a villain. Billing also genuinely loves Miss Mansfield. In other words, Billing is a complex person. Draw up a chart of the 'good' and 'bad' features of one of the main characters in the book as part of a discussion on the nature of 'goodness' and 'badness'.

Chapter twenty summary	Language features	Links in and beyond the book
Mr. Field's fortune is found hidden in the graveyard. Smith is given ten thousand guineas, which overwhelms his sisters. Billing returns and turns State evidence— and is murdered in Newgate by a crazy old man. The sisters become court dress-makers. Miss Mansfield marries happily. Smith becomes the magistrate's loyal and affectionate companion.		* Fairy story 'and they all lived happily ever after' endings.

Chapter twenty possible activities

A.   The old man in the grate murders Billing, but we are not told why. Invent your own tale of the life of the old man and tell it either as the old man himself (see chapter 10 for a description of him) or through the eyes of his neat hangman son (see chapter 3 for a brief description of him).

B.   The book has a neat and tidy, 'happy ever after' ending for some characters, but what happens to the second man in brown, the old servant Andrews, Mr. Field's sister and nephews, Meg the scullerymaid? Tell the tale of what happens to one of them next, as far as possible keeping to the style of the book.

C.   Smith is now 'neat' and 'small'. Go back to the very start of the novel and look at the original Smith. Explain which Smith you would rather be and why.

D.   Imagine Smith a year later. Set down his thoughts in his not-so-novel life in a diary or in a letter to Miss Mansfield or in a chat with Meg the scullerymaid.

E.   The chapter opens with the weather echoing the mood of everything now being wonderful. Rewrite the scene on a day when Smith is feeling rather less content.

F.   Smith comes into a small fortune. Have a 'brainstorm' session on what people would like to spend such money on!

Appendix 2

Working on an aspect—book illustration

Working for a while on the pictorial components of prose fiction is not a 'babyish' thing to do. It can create a classroom climate in which pupils can be open about their interests and tastes across a wide range of material, and through which they can look at their development as readers and the development of others close to them.

Because such a topic relies extensively on the visual, less literate and less motivated readers have a chance of getting involved and of having contributions to make. At the same time, the constant and obvious technique of comparing, contrasting or linking illustration and text can set up discussion and other work on what techniques an artist can call upon, their limitations and potential; what techniques an author can exploit, their limitations and potential; the interplay of the two.

The strategies and tactics set out here are illustrations of ways of working rather than a set recipe. It will certainly repay you to adapt rather than adopt. Some teachers prefer to run a 'unit' on such a topic, for a fortnight, a month or even longer; others prefer to use an idea when the moment seems right. Whichever appeals to you, it will be worth looking at Elaine Moss's *Picture Books for Young People* (Signal Books) for further ideas and for a very useful, annotated list of picture books.

Preparation

It is worth spending a small amount of time sorting out ideas and materials for this project. Several sources can be helpful, in a variety of ways:

1 *School librarian*—is worth consulting about relevant stock and about the possibility of having a temporary 'mini-library' in the library or in your classroom.
2 *Local library*—is often enthusiastic about such work, especially if you can contact its children's or youth librarian. The library should be able to help you sort out background reading for yourself and give you information on any expertise in your area, e.g. a book illustrator or a printing or publishing firm. It may also be able to provide a special project loan, including picture books for young children.

3 *School art department*—may have some expertise to offer and may be prepared to liaise on the project, e.g. a 'visiting speaker' from the art department; pupils working on book illustrations in 'art' time.

4 *Regional arts association*—should be able to advise you on worthwhile authors and artists and should be able to subsidize their coming to your school. The local association's address is available from your local library.

5 *Publishers*—can be helpful over publicity material, including book-jackets and posters. (See *Appendix 7* for useful addresses.)

6 *Newsagents*—may sometimes give you old magazines, a useful source of material for comparing the variety of ways in which illustration and story can interact.

It is also worth getting a stock of the sorts of texts you want to work on, just in case other sources, including the pupils themselves, do not prove very forthcoming.

Teaching

The sequence of ideas presented here is not sacrosanct. You may want to change it or simply adopt and adapt one or two of its ideas for your own purposes.

1
As a 'trailer' to the project, bring in a few picture books and childhood publications. You may or may not need to use one or two of these in order to encourage a chat session about childhood memories of books and reading and being read to, bringing in the topic of illustrations, whatever their context. The more anecdotal and non-judgmental the session is, the better. Feed in a *few* of your own memories as part of creating a sharing climate and to ensure that the topic of memories and reactions concerning illustrations crops up.

2
Arrange for a class 'museum' of childhood books, maybe using some stock from the local library alongside stock which you, staff colleagues and pupils contribute. Nobody should contribute a book which is genuinely rare or particularly precious, and the 'museum' should be for supervised reference use. That is easier if the stock can be kept in your class base, but if you are forced to be a nomadic teacher you will probably have to keep the collection in a box or cupboard between sessions. Use the stock for quiet reading time and for group discussion. Bringers (including staff) can provide brief anecdotes about their books and how their stories and pictures moved or disappointed them in their younger days. Others can

comment on how they respond to the pictures now—and how they would expect contemporary young children to respond to them. Such work can take place in one long session or over three or four shorter, more incidental ones, as the books come trickling in. In either case, it remains important to keep up an exploratory, appreciative atmosphere.

3

Hold a session on the historical aspect of book illustration. One way to do this is to read a small selection of tales or episodes, with the pupils listening, deciding which point in the text should be illustrated and how. Looking at the illustrations can then lead to some spirited discussion in the degree of match or mismatch! Fairy stories can be one way in, for instance *The Sleeping Beauty*. Looking at the Ladybird Books version and the version in Iona and Peter Opie's *The Classic Fairy Tales* (Oxford, 1974) makes a very useful contrast. (In olden days, Sleeping Beauty was *not* woken with a kiss!) It is also worth going for popular books, so that you have a chance of getting more than one copy, thus diminishing problems over seeing the illustrations. If you have some means of projection and can take slides, for example of Victorian or Edwardian illustrations, so much the better. It is possible to pick up Victorian or Edwardian children's fiction quite reasonably. Its illustrations generate interesting comment on text-picture links then and now.

4

It is worth harnessing the pupils' own experience of childhood reading for more detailed consideration. One way is to work 'developmentally', starting with books for the very young and working through to 'older' books which the pupils used to read (and may still do). These can range from Mr. Men to Beatrix Potter to Enid Blyton, for example. A second is to tackle illustrations under various headings: one group can look at how animals are depicted, another at girls, another at boys, another at parents, at other adults, at various ethnic groups, at moments of crisis, at school/domestic/country settings, and so on. Each group can produce an illustrated mini-lecture for the rest. One illustration may be the object of inquiry of more than one group, a handy means of getting some focused discussion. In every instance, pupils should be encouraged to go to the story itself to support any comment they want to make about its illustration.

5

Look at the latest illustrated books where the illustrations are present to support the text. (If possible, link with your local library, so that the stock is really new and so that school and library are seen as natural partners.) Again, expect any discussion about bookjackets or internal illustrations to be backed up by at least 'dip' reference to the book itself. One idea is to have a display of new books and get pupils to say which covers are the most attractive—and what they think, having dipped into the first chapter or so.

6

There are texts in which illustrations are at least as important as words, or even replace them. One way to look at this is to discuss 'pure' picture books. Another is to turn to comics. This can be a rich source of work, especially if you can obtain some old comics for contrastive purposes. Discussion can look at the interdependence of pictures and text; what the pictures carry as information which the words do not; what words would have to be written, if the pictures were taken away (an interesting exercise on narrative techniques and on authorial commentary); on how 'economical' words and pictures have to be in the brevity of tales in comics (a link with the economy of telling necessary in short stories); on the special language of comics; on visual stereotype and cliché and how far these are to be found, through group study of 'comic' comics, 'love' comics and 'war' comics; on what audiences comics seem to aim to attract.

The ideas above can be linked through a topic on the conventions and techniques of book illustration over the years. This area of accepted styles and conventions might well attract a member of your art department and be the focus for some linked teaching.

The relationship of illustration to text is worth discussing, including the frequency and siting of illustrations and their quality as responses to highlights or action or character interplay or setting in the story. The intention of the illustration, to be literal or to be evocative, should also be discussed.

An examination of techniques used and the literary, artistic, technical and commercial factors affecting their choice can prove interesting. For example, adventure stories in the early 1900s often used photographic half-tone plates of artists' impressions of a scene—a form of emotional narrative illustration developed by the late Victorians. Enid Blyton's books usually contain line drawings which give very little information by way of age or characterization or character relationships, a significant point in discussing her books. Charles Keeping's complex drawings also rely upon line but have an intense, almost dæmonic quality as they take upon themselves the right not to interpret literally but to respond to the text through the eyes and hands of a complex and deeply engaged reader-artist. For example, see his illustrations for L. Garfield and E. Blishen's *God Beneath the Sea* (Longman, 1970) or for Alfred Noyes' *The Highwayman* or Kevin Crossley-Holland's *Beowulf* (Oxford 1982 and 1983).

Throughout, discussion of which pictures 'fit' books or do not—and why—helps to focus on the least tangible of a book's qualities, its 'flavour'. Sometimes, getting pupils to consider whether the illustrations within a book or on its jacket give a picture of the book as they themselves have come to see it helps them to think about the novel's essential qualities and features—and, perhaps, to recreate the book in their mind's eye.

7

Using insights from the work on comics, look at books in which the illustrations are as important as the words, starting with books for the very young. (Pupils may contribute some, together with their memories of them. Try to get some recent ones, perhaps on loan from the local library, so that points of continuity and change can be considered.) The topics listed in **6** can be used here, but there are more—how characters are created and differentiated; how, perhaps, they are shown to change; what challenges they meet and how they respond; whether the author makes a running commentary or tries to keep out of the tale; whether the artist makes comments, and if so, how; in the case of an author-artist, whether one medium is more important than the other.

If this work succeeds, pupils can become very involved in producing their own books for young readers, sorting out what seem to be the most popular topics by looking at books and talking to children and deciding what features and sorts of illustration appeal most to young readers. This can be an excellent occasion for liaison between the English and art departments and between a secondary and an infants school, especially when the finished books are taken down to the infant school to be read by their authors to two or three children and, maybe, to be lodged there.

8

This can lead to consideration of illustrated texts for the less young—Hergés *Adventures of Tin Tin*, for example, and the humour of the *Astérix* series. Another approach is to look at the work of one person. One compact series for such study is the work of Raymond Briggs, ranging from his *Father Christmas* texts through *Fungus the Bogeyman* and *Gentleman Jim* to *When the Wind Blows*. Text and illustration both yield much for discussion about how an artist-author works, what interests or obsesses him, and how he develops. There are other artist-authors, for example Charles Keeping and Maurice Sendak, but Briggs promotes a lot of ideas, although some teachers might want to avoid *When the Wind Blows* and its topic of a nuclear holocaust. It is important to look at his books before you use them, as with any other work. Certainly, his books are avidly read in those schools which have copies of them.

9

Pupils can return to books for their own age, looking at a class text and deciding which moments should be illustrated, setting out 'working notes' for an artist on what the illustrations should contain, what form they should take and why. Discussion about their choice is likely to make explicit what, to them, are the important moments of the text—a handy means of helping you to get some idea of their versions of what the book is about and to see what its language has conveyed to them and how that has occurred.

10

If funds allow, one further device is to read a text and to have groups working out how some of its episodes might be realized in a film, following this up with a showing of the film of the book. Examples include the films of James Vance Marshall's *Walkabout*, Jack Schaeffer's *Shane*, George Orwell's *Animal Farm* and William Golding's *Lord of the Flies*.

Background reading

1 *History*
Eyre F. *British Children's Books in the Twentieth Century*, Longman, 1971.
Feaver W. *When We Were Young*, Thames & Hudson, 1971.
2 *Illustrators*
Culpan N. & Waite C. *Variety is King* (Section 6), Longman, 1977.
Egoff S. et al. *Only Connect* (Section 9), Oxford, 1980.
3 *Illustrations*
Peppin B. *Fantasy: Book Illustration 1860–1920*, Studio Vista, 1975.
Larkin D. *Arthur Rackham*, Pan, 1975.
Larkin D. *Edmund Dulac*, Coronet, 1975.
4 *Comics*
Gifford D. *Happy Days: A Century of Comics*, Jupiter Books, 1975.
Perry G. *The Penguin Book of Comics*, Penguin, 1971.
5 *Other Sources*
See the Weston Woods catalogue for details. (Address in Appendix 7.)

Possible illustrated books and illustrators

See Elaine Moss's book for detailed recommendations. Consider also:
Fiction in the *Ladybird* series
Roger Hargreaves's *Mr Men* series
Tomi Ungerer *The Three Robbers*
John Burningham's *Cannonball Simp*, etc.
Brian Wildsmith
Allan Ahlberg's *Funnybones*
Maurice Sendak's *Where the Wild Things Are*, etc.
Edward Ardizzone
Newspaper series, such as *Rupert*
Wayne Anderson and Christopher Logue's *Ratsmagic*
Hergé's *Tin Tin* series
Goscinny and Uderzo's *Astérix* series
Series by Enid Blyton, Arthur Ransome, etc.
Raymond Briggs
Charles Keeping

Appendix 3

The thematic approach: Islands

Extracts of related books, selected for their portrayal of one theme from different viewpoints, used to be more popular than at present. The approach has been criticized because the works are presented as fragments, losing their total impact, but this need not be the case if the books used are part of a class library or are otherwise available for the class to read independently. Extracts then become 'tasters' to encourage wider reading. There are many other advantages to the approach. It offers variety, contrasting with the in-depth study of one book at a time; it makes pupils more aware of alternative viewpoints and styles through the contrast of similar occurrences; it provides a greater variety of models for pupils' own writing.

An alternative to the class library is the theme box, containing small sets or single copies of a variety of texts, perhaps including non-fiction, for a range of reading abilities. This last point is especially important in mixed ability work, and the thematic approach does allow for pupils of all abilities to be involved, if a range of books can be found. Assignment sheets can be related to the books in the box. To allow for different abilities, the first part of the sheet should have a limited number of straightforward questions concerned with the text or personal experiences, for 'starters'. A second section might concern more complex issues, such as relationships between characters or plot development. A third section might encourage wider reading—comparing the target text with others—or personal writing, either reflective or pastiche. This is not to suggest that only the brightest pupils should be allowed to progress to the final section. If the 'starters' are brief, then all pupils should be able to tackle some part of the other sections. The important thing is to allow for differing abilities by not making all pupils work through the same sequence of questions; indeed, wherever possible let them make their own choice within each section.

The example which follows is of a theme suitable for lower to middle secondary: *Islands*. There are many books available, particularly if 'island as metaphor' is taken into account. The first stage in planning a theme might be to draw up a list of suitable books. Some local libraries have a schools' service which will make up a thematic box, either to order or making a selection on your behalf. The second stage is to draw up a concept map of possibilities which might arise out of those texts, and obviously it is essential to know the material well enough to be able to make this map. The third stage is to select from the map the most promising components for a teaching sequence, considering ways of involving pupils actively in a) talking b) writing c) drama d) literary appreciation. Examples of these three stages follow:

1 Book selection: Island theme

1)	Ballantyne R.M.	*Coral Island*
2)	Defoe D.	*Robinson Crusoe*
3)	Durrell G.	*My Family and Other Animals*
4)	Fisk N.	*High Way Home*
5)	Golding W.	*Lord of the Flies*
		Pincher Martin
6)	Grimble A.	*A Pattern of Islands*
7)	Huxley A.	*Island*
8)	Jansson T.	*The Summer Book*
9)	Le Guin U.	*Wizard of Earthsea*
10)	Mark J.	*The Ennead*
11)	Neal T.	*An Island to Oneself*
12)	O'Dell S.	*Island of the Blue Dolphins*
13)	Stephenson R.L.	*Treasure Island*
14)	Taylor T.	*The Cay*
15)	Twain M.	*Huckleberry Finn*
16)	Wells H.G.	*The Island of Dr. Moreau*
17)	Wilder L.I.	*Little House on the Prairie*

2 A Concept map (numbers refer to titles in book selection)

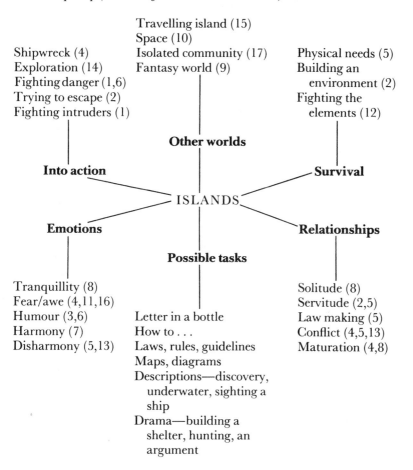

Travelling island (15)
Space (10)
Isolated community (17)
Fantasy world (9)

Shipwreck (4)
Exploration (14)
Fighting danger (1,6)
Trying to escape (2)
Fighting intruders (1)

Physical needs (5)
Building an
  environment (2)
Fighting the
  elements (12)

Other worlds

Into action   **Survival**

ISLANDS

Emotions   **Relationships**

Possible tasks

Tranquillity (8)
Fear/awe (4,11,16)
Humour (3,6)
Harmony (7)
Disharmony (5,13)

Solitude (8)
Servitude (2,5)
Law making (5)
Conflict (4,5,13)
Maturation (4,8)

Letter in a bottle
How to . . .
Laws, rules, guidelines
Maps, diagrams
Descriptions—discovery,
  underwater, sighting a
  ship
Drama—building a
  shelter, hunting, an
  argument

3 Teaching sequence: activities arising from given extracts
Shipwreck (*High Way Home* pp 25–29). Exploration (*Lord of the Flies* ch. 1).
Building a shelter (*Robinson Crusoe* ch. 4 cf. *The Cay* ch. 8). Finding food
(*Pincher Martin* ch. 5 cf. *Lord of the Flies* ch. 9).

Talking: fear of water, power of the elements, sense impressions of
swimming. How to build shelters: likely materials. Food essential for
survival.

Writing: sense impression description or interior monologue of shipwreck.
Contrastive paragraphs—fighting for life in surf, then walking on beautiful
beach.

Drama: solo work on slow motion fighting to control ship, swimming, then walking on beach. Pair work on exploring—through jungle, across swamp, over rocks. Pair work on building shelters, lighting fire, cooking food.

Literary Focus: first person narrative; sense impression writing; establishment of setting.

The above would be the first phase of work on a theme, which can continue by exploring the concepts of a) emotional states; b) danger; c) attempting to escape, or going into relationships—perhaps developing a community on the island in successive stages—or into 'other worlds'.

Appendix 4

A project on a novel

This book has set out to outline current practice which engages pupils as active readers. This appendix was devised by Kim Redshaw who explains its outline and purpose for himself.

Brave New World by Aldous Huxley

The material on *Brave New World* came from the belief that people learn things better and with more understanding by finding out for themselves rather than being told. The various research items and creative pieces included in the material were of the sort I used in English classes throughout the secondary school age range in working with fiction. In this case, the material was designed specifically for a fifth year group of thirty pupils tackling GCE 'O' level literature in a Norfolk comprehensive school, preparing for the Cambridge Board Plain Texts Paper. Had I been teaching them for a more traditional paper, I would have prepared the material in the same way.

The pupils worked on the material for about six weeks. Some of the time each week was spent on drama, mainly improvisations concerned with specific themes from the novel such as 'conditioning' and with generally illustrating aspects of life in the 'new world'.

The research items were done individually and in groups. Everybody did Item 1. Six groups were formed for Item 2. Each group researched one character and produced its findings, which were written up on a banda master sheet by a scribe from each group. I duplicated a copy for all members of the class to check through the information and, using the banda sheet as a basis, to produce their own personal notes on each character. A similar system was used for Item 8, where each member of the class was responsible for checking through seven pages of the novel, searching for 'slogans' and adding them to a banda master sheet ready for duplication. Everyone did 3 and 9 on their own. Five groups were formed for 4, 5, 6, 7 and 10. Each group researched its assigned topic, subdividing within the group as members thought fit before bringing their information together in a report which was duplicated for the rest of the form. These reports were signed by the members of the group who had written them. On receipt of these, individuals presented any queries they had to the writers themselves. From such queries, changes were made and announced to everyone. These were very interesting sessions. The research activities produced a good collective feeling and a strong sense of responsibility in each group, which felt bound to produce a good report for the others. I don't necessarily recommend doing the research in this way, I merely point it out. Time was a factor.

The creative items were important, too. They were done individually for the most part. Some collaborated over writing scripts. Everyone tried to do at least four pieces—one from 1-4; one from 5a-5i, one from 6a-6g and one from 7a-7d. Once again, time was a factor and not everyone finished. But the work was good and everyone learned a lot about Huxley's *Brave New World*.

Research work

1 The plot
On *one* sheet of paper—it may be quite large—display in a visually interesting and forceful way the essential storyline, chapter by chapter.

2 The Main Characters
Bernard, John 'the Savage', Lenina, Mustapha Mond, Linda, Helmholtz. For each, note:
>   **a** physical appearance
>   **b** first appearance in book
>   **c** what he/she says
>   (some typical quotes, perhaps)
>   **d** what he/she thinks
>   **e** how he/she acts in moments of stress, anger, emotion or danger
>   **f** what others say or think of him/her
>   **g** whether he/she changes

Present the information in a visually interesting way, e.g. the page of a police profile for each or an encyclopaedia entry for each (*Who's Who?*) or enlarged passport information, etc.

3 The History of Brave New World
Using information from anywhere in the book but mainly chapter three, present in note form a clear potted history of the world from the twentieth century to the time in which the novel is set. Present this information in a visually interesting way.

4 A list of terms
Find out the meanings of the following terms. Give a definition in one or two lines, if possible.

Anthrax bomb
Bokanovsky Process
Bottling
Centrifugal Bumble-Puppy
Community Sing
Ectogenesis
Emotional Engineering
Erotic Play
Feelies
Five Step
Ford
Freemartin
Hypnopaedia
Malthusian Belt
Orgy-Porgy
Pneumatic
Podsnap's Technique
Pregnancy Substitute
Scent and Color Organ
Sexaphone
Sex-hormone Chewing Gum
Social Predestination
Solidarity Service
Soma
Super-Vox-Wurlitzeriana
Surrogate

Present your list as interestingly as possible.

5 Conditioning, the caste system and population control
Divide a page in two. On the left, state important characteristics of *Brave New World* which are different from our own. On the right, say why someone who believes in the new society like Mustapha Mond would say they are good things. See especially ch.1, 2, 3, 16, 17.

Caste system (Mond,ch16,p182)	It is good to produce people happy to do their appropriate type of work rather than

6 Religion and Ford
Collect and note references to and explanations of Ford and of any ceremonies and beliefs connected with this. See for example chapter two. Present the notes in a visually interesting way.

7 Love and sexual relationships
Collect and note some examples of the 'B.N.W.' attitudes towards love and sex. See, among other examples, John's worship of Lenina in chapter nine and his disgust for her in chapter thirteen. Try to present these notes in a visually interesting way.

8 Slogans
Collect as many slogans as you can and make a note of them—for example:

> Ending is better than mending. The more stitches the less riches.
> Cleanliness is next to fordliness.
> Civilization is sterilization.

Display them as powerfully as possible, e.g. as graffiti on a large sheet of paper sketched to resemble a brick wall.

9 The 1946 Foreword (See pages xiii-xxi)
Read Huxley's 1946 Foreword carefully. Make a note of anything of importance or interest in it, for example:

> He says that if he were to rewrite the book he would give the savage more than two choices at the end.
> He talks about the accuracy of the prophecies in the book.

10 Irony and Satire
Make a note of examples you can find in the book of Huxley satirizing our society or satirizing the 'Brave New World' society for believing it can solve problems at the expense of emotions and feelings.
Look for examples of where the following are satirized:

> the glorification of science and medicine
> the desire of mankind for conformity
> present day religious institutions and ceremonies
> present day and 'new world' organized entertainment
> attitudes to death
> the desire of mankind to be ruled by a strict, authoritarian regime.

Creative pieces

1 News broadcasts
Script an edition of 'The News at Ten' from the B.N.W. Broadcasting Corporation. Base some items on incidents from the book. Others will be 'fictional' but should use information and background from the novel.

2 Newspaper items
a Create the front page for the B.N.W. state newspaper, based on at least

one actual incident in the book. This should be the headline story. Other items can be made up.

b Create a collection of supposed newspaper cuttings to cover the time-scale of the book. Many of these cuttings will be about actual incidents in the book; some will be made up through using information and background material from the book. Write each one to column shapes, cut them out and stick them in to make them look like a collection of cuttings in a scrap book.

3 Quiz
Make up a quiz concerned with events in the book. Provide answers. Vary the questions—some easy and a few very hard.

4 Crossword
Compile a crossword using people and events and terms used in the novel.

5 Script ideas
a Script a radio programme which intends to promote interest in the book. Include one or two dramatized excerpts. Put at least part of it on tape.
b Write a script for acting via film or radio of an episode in the book—of one chapter, perhaps.
c Script a 'phone-in' programme with calls to the characters in the book, asking about their motives, actions and attitudes. The author could be asked questions as well, or could be the subject of a separate 'phone-in'.
d Script a 'post mortem' conversation among the main characters, who discuss the parts they have played in the novel. Characters have the chance to challenge the actions of other characters. Discussion should be consistent with the text.
e Work out an improvisation outline for the whole—or part—of the book.
f Script one or a series of interviews between a TV interviewer and a leading character about the character's actions in the book.
g Work out a complete drama script (half hour or less) which, in a telescoped way, covers the action of the whole book.
h Using chapter four as a basis, script a piece of dialogue between Bernard and Helmholtz so that each shows how he feels about himself and about the state.
i Script the scene between John and Lenina in chapter thirteen. Make it short but complete. Try to bring out clearly what each is feeling.

6 Diary entries, letters and pieces of personal reminiscence
a Of one of the students being shown round in chapter one.
b Of the student in chapter two who can see that reading wastes time but doesn't understand why people are conditioned to dislike flowers.

c Of someone watching the formal games in chapter three, surprised to hear that erotic play used to be considered abnormal.

d Of Lenina describing her evening at the cabaret with Henry in chapter five.

e Of Bernard describing his thoughts about the Brave New World and the reservation. Base this on material from chapter six.

f Of Lenina describing the reservation, Linda and John. Base this on material from chapter seven.

g Of John recording his personal reactions to the New World to which he has been brought.

7 Visual presentations

a *A poster* Design a poster or a series of posters for the book or the film of the book or some posters that the Brave New World Government might issue to warn or encourage its people.

b *Book cover* Design a back and front cover for the novel.

c *Illustrations.* Do one or two or a series of illustrations for scenes from the novel. Include the appropriate quotation at the bottom of each illustration.

d *Cartoons* Draw a strip cartoon version of one or two chapters. (Use matchstick men, if you find drawing hard.)

Appendix 5

Addresses

You will find extensive lists of addresses in *Children's Books: An Information Guide*, published by the Centre for Children's Books. The brief list below provides some of the more commonly needed addresses.

Arts Council of Great Britain
105 Piccadilly, London W1V 0AU, 01 629 9495.

> If you want to make use of the 'Writers in Schools' scheme and cannot find the address of your Regional Arts Association, the Arts Council will supply it. Teachers in Scotland should write to The Scottish Arts Council at 19 Charlotte Square, Edinburgh EH2 49F. Teachers in Wales should write to The Welsh Arts Council at Holst House, 9 Museum Place, Cardiff CF1 3NX.

Centre for Children's Books
National Book League, Book House, 45 East Hill, London SW18 2QZ, 01 870 9055.

> This is *the* national information centre and powerhouse, as far as children's fiction is concerned. Its full range of services and publications are to be found in its indispensable *Children's Books: An Information Guide*. The Centre holds a stock of the last two years' children's fiction as a reference library.

Commission for Racial Equality
Elliott House, 10-12 Allington Street, London SW1E 5EH, 01 828 7022.

> Handy for advice, for its checklist on 'Racism and Sexism in Books' and for its list of specialist bookshops.

The Library Association
7 Ridgmount Street, London WC1E 7AE, 01 636 7543.

> Important for its lively Youth Libraries Group and its publications.

National Association for the Teaching of English
NATE Office, 49 Broomgrove Road, Sheffield S10 2NA, 0742 683924.

> Important as the national organization for *all* interested in teaching English. Interesting journal and annual national conference. Check with the Sheffield address to see if there is a NATE Branch near you which you can join as part of your 'grapevine'.

Publishers' Association
19 Bedford Square, London WC1B 3HJ, 01 580 6321-5.

> The Association can supply a list of publishers of children's books and will provide advice if you would like to take part in the annual National Children's Book Week. Its Home Trade Secretary can advise on legal aspects of running a school bookshop.

The School Bookshop Association
1 Effingham Road, Lee, London SE12 8NZ, 01 852 4953.

This should be your first port of call if you are thinking of starting a school bookshop. It will provide sensible and enthusiastic support and advice. Its handbook *How to set up and run a school bookshop* is particularly recommended.

You may well wish to start up a bookshop with the help of a local shop or supplier. If you do not—or you are miles from a bookshop—look at what various firms have to offer, for example Books for Students Ltd., 58-64 Berrington Road, Sydenham Industrial Estate, Leamington Spa CV31 1BR. Some teachers prefer to use one of the postal book clubs available to schools. Again, shop around. Firms include Read On!, Napier Place, Cumbernauld, Glasgow G68 0DN and Scholastic Book Clubs, Scholastic Publications Ltd., Westfield Road, Southam, Nr. Leamington Spa CV33 0BR.

School Library Association
Victoria House, 29-31 George Street, Oxford OX1 2AY, 0865 722746.

This is a long-established, experienced organization, producing a range of practical pamphlets on school library organization and on books for children and a journal known for its full and independent reviews of children's fiction. The National Secretary can tell you if there is a branch near you which could be a useful part of your 'grapevine' of information and contacts.

Schools Broadcasting Council for the United Kingdom
The Langham, Portland Place, London W1A 1AA, 01 580 4468.

The Council can supply the annual programme of BBC radio and television broadcasts to schools. If you want details of ITV school transmissions, you should contact your regional ITV company. Both organizations have regional education officers.

Appendix 6

Books and journals

Of the making of books about children and their books there is no end. This is a brief sample of some of the resources available. It has six sections:

1 **Background** Books of general interest on children's fiction.
2 **Bibliographies** Selections of children's fiction which may be of use in choosing books for the library or the classroom.
3 **Journals** Journals on children's fiction, teaching English and on library organization.
4 **Libraries** Books on library practice.
5 **Teaching** Books on teaching English and the role of fiction.
6 **Teenagers** Books on teenage reading tastes and on teenage fiction.

1 Background

Centre for Children's Books. *Children's Books: An Information Guide*, Centre for Children's Books, Book House, 45 East Hill, London SW18 2Q2.

If you buy nothing else, buy this, for it is full of information on every aspect of books for children and on where to go for more.

Applebee A. *The Child's Concept of Story (2-17)*, University of Chicago, 1978.

Story readers are also story makers. This is an expensive but important book for anyone wanting to look at recent work on how a young reader develops a 'storying' ability.

Herhardt L. *Issues on Children's Book Selection*, R. R. Bowker & Co., New York, 1973.

Section Three is interesting for its transatlantic articles on 'images' in fiction of Blacks, Jews and Native Americans and the issues of sexism and feminism.

Hildick W. *Children and Fiction*, Evans, 1970.

A lively, provocative book by a writer of children's fiction, setting out the artistic and psychological factors which affect writing for this audience. You may also enjoy Joan Aiken's *The Way to Write for Children* published by Elm Tree Books (1982).

Ingham J. *Books and Reading Development: The Bradford Book Flood Experiment*, Heinemann Educational Books, 1981.

This study found that 'flooding' a school with books could decrease reading—unless there was time for personal reading in school and unless there was access to informed, enthusiastic teachers who could gossip and accept gossip about books. Pupils liked books that they already had some idea about, perhaps introduced by the teacher as reader-sharer, by peers or by the media. Book reading records increased awareness of books and provided common ground for the conversation of pupils and teachers. The 'flood' took place in middle schools but much of what the book has to say is equally relevant to work with secondary school pupils.

Inglis F. *The Promise of Happiness: Value and Meaning in Children's Fiction*, Cambridge, 1981.

In some ways an impassioned book, presenting the author's views on the best children's fiction of the century and on the social values it explores.

Iser W. *The Act of Reading: A Theory of Aesthetic Response*, Routledge & Kegan Paul, 1978.

This is an advanced text, exploring how text and reader interact and how the reader has to carry out the book's 'instructions' in assembling its 'meaning'.

Jones C. & Klein G. *Assessing Children's Books for a Multi-Ethnic Society: Practical Guidelines for Primary and Secondary Schools*, London, 1981.

A practical, brief checklist of eight items plus useful addresses and suggestions for further reading. Available from The Library, Centre for Urban Educational Studies, 34 Aberdeen Park, London N5 2BL.

Kirkpatrick D. (ed). *Twentieth Century Children's Writers,* Macmillan, 1978.

A mammoth tome of critical essays and bibliographies by various writers on this century's authors for children. Worth consulting at your local library if you want to check up on an author.

Meek M., Warlow A. & Barton G. (eds). *The Cool Web: The Pattern of Children's Reading*, Bodley Head, 1977.

An essential, comprehensive book, containing the evidence submitted to the Bullock Report committee on children and fiction. Its fifty or so papers provide a wide perspective, but look particularly at Hardy, Harding, Britton and Gregory.

Stinton J. (ed). *Racism and Sexism in Children's Books* (2nd edn), Writers and Readers Publishing Co-operative, London, 1979.

An interesting collection of articles on the 'images' generated in children's books. See Herhardt's book for an American view of the topic.

Townsend J. R. *Written for Children*, Kestrel Books, London, 1974.

A lightly handled outline of the history of children's literature in English, looking at books published in England, the Commonwealth and the United States. An enjoyable background book.

Tucker N. *The Child and the Book: A Psychological and Literary Exploration*, CUP, 1981.

A clear, coherent overview of the child as a developing reader, full of easily handled scholarship. The book tackles a range of topics and issues from Enid Blyton to censorship, and has some interesting views on why some pupils like reading and some do not.

2 Bibliographies

Ballin R., Bleach J. & Levine J. *A Wider Heritage: A Selection of Books for Children and Young People in Multicultural Britain*, National Book League, London, 1980.

Detailed summaries of over a hundred books for the secondary age range, with information on other bibliographies, journals, specialist bookshops, publishers and suppliers.

Brownhill S. *Starting Point: Books for the Illiterate Adult and Older Reluctant Reader* (3rd edn), National Book League, London, 1979.

A fairly detailed review of most of the series written specifically for the 'weak' reader. Such books can sometimes be useful as starting points, provided that they are not the only fiction a reader encounters.

Commonwealth Institute. *Commonwealth Children's Literature*, Commonwealth Institute, London.

A list of books from throughout the Commonwealth—potentially interesting but there is no comment on what the books are about.

Dixon B. *Now Read On: Recommended Fiction for Young People—Good Books with Positive Attitudes to Sex, Race, Class and Other Issues*, Pluto Press, London, 1982.

Quite a title for a committed, lively book which should question and clarify some of your own ideas. Two hundred titles are discussed, some recent, but some old friends seen anew.

Frend P. *Junior Fiction Index* (4th edn), Association of Assistant Librarians, 1981.

An encyclopaedic list of fiction for readers up to the age of sixteen. There is no suggested reading age or commentary on individual titles, but books are clustered alphabetically under topic headings. If you want fiction involving autism, avalanches or Aztecs, this is where you start. Worth borrowing from your local library or buying in your consortium of schools.

Kloet C. *Reading for Enjoyment: 12 Years Old and Up*, Baker Book Services, 1981.

A detailed list of just over one hundred titles which the selector has found teenagers do enjoy. The books are available as an exhibition from the National Book League. See also Ann Bartholomew's *Reading for Enjoyment 7-11 Year Olds* in the same series. Both can be bought from the Centre for Children's Books.

Mears J. & Parker A. *Read Aloud to 7-13 Year Olds*, Library Association Youth Libraries Group, 1974.

Perhaps a little out of date, but a useful annotated list of books which teachers have found successful as classroom serial readers. Worth looking at as a preliminary to collaborating with teachers in your area on a list of classroom novels which 'work'.

Moss E. *Picture Books for Young People 9-13*, Signal Books, 1981.

'The new picture book is a demanding medium: it makes the reader think; it encourages discussion in groups.' Detailed commentary on over eighty picture books shows that they can have a definite role in looking at fiction, providing centres of debate in mixed ability classes. Interesting categories include 'A Wry Look at Ourselves' and 'A Deep Look at Ourselves'.

Salway L. *Humorous Books for Children* (2nd edn), Signal Books, 1978.

An avowedly individual, enthusiastic list which may help to clarify your own thinking on this topic and widen the range of texts in your library.

Smyth M. *Count Me In: Books for and about Disabled Children*, Library Association Youth Libraries Group, 1981.

An interesting list, chosen to promote greater insight into the nature of various forms of handicap and fuller understanding of those who have problems because of them.

Sherrard-Smith B. *Children's Books of the Year '81*, Julia MacRae/National Book League, 1982.

Children's Books of the Year provides full, informed reviews of fiction and non-fiction. It is well worth consulting, especially when getting in new library stock, as is *The Signal Review of Children's Books*, edited by Nancy Chambers and published by The Thimble Press.

Townsend J. R. *Twenty Five Years of British Children's Books*, National Book League, 1977.

> An annotated list of some two hundred books. Worth looking at because of the selector's criterion that they 'should not require more experience of life or of other literature than children can reasonably be expected to have.' Age ranges are given.

Warren D. *Fiction, Verse and Legend for Middle and Secondary Schools* (2nd edn), School Library Association, 1978.

> An interesting list of some nine hundred books under such categories as General, Historical Settings, School Background, Animal Interest, Science Fiction and Fantasy. Sensible comments throughout.

3 Journals

Bookpage. 10 Westside, Fortis Green, London N2 9ES.

> This is an interesting venture. Each issue contains information on twenty *recent* books—usually paperbacks—reviewed on A4 sheets under a series of headings which make lighter work for the teacher. An accompanying A4 sheet on each book sets out questions for pupils to solve about the book and suggestions for further, more responsive work. Details of availability and subscription rates are available from Peter Hyams at the above address.

Books for Keeps. School Bookshop Association, 1 Effingham Road, Lee, London SE12 8NZ.

> A lively, wide-ranging journal, with reviews that range from the enthusiastic to the trenchant. Features include articles on authors and illustrators and useful news on book-radio/television/film links, so that you have time to prepare to exploit them. The 'magazine' style attracts pupils as well as teachers. Six issues a year. Recommended.

British Book News—Children's Book Supplement. British Council/Heffer's Children's Bookshop, 30 Trinity Street, Cambridge CB2 1TB.

> The spring and autumn issues of *British Book News* contain annotated lists of children's fiction, set out under age groups, providing handy half-yearly sumaries of new books.

Children's Book Bulletin. Children's Rights Workshop, 4 Aldebert Terrace, London SW8 1BH.

> A journal on 'progressive moves in children's literature' including books for a multi-ethnic, non-sexist society. It has some lively independent reviews which do not necessarily praise 'accepted' authors. Three issues a year.

Children's Literature in Education. 2 Sunwine Place, Exmouth, Devon.

> An international journal with a high reputation. Articles on classroom practice, the nature of literary response and on bibliographies of fiction for schools appear alongside articles by or about famous authors and illustrators. Four issues a year.

English in Education. N.A.T.E. office, 49 Broomgrove Road, Sheffield S10 2NA.

> The termly journal of the National Association for the Teaching of English is essential reading for teachers considering all aspects of the subject. It has been notable for articles on classroom practice and on finding out how pupils really do respond.

The English Magazine. ILEA English Centre (Magazine), Sutherland Street, London SW1.

A lively, practical journal on every aspect of English teaching. Has had useful reviews on fiction which has proved effective in the classroom or library and surveys on the out-of-school reading of teenage boys and girls. Three issues a year. Recommended.

Essex Review of Children's Literature. S.E. Essex Teachers' Centre, Hadleigh, Essex.

Nicholas Tucker has long argued that the most useful reviews of children's fiction must include contributions by teachers, with their knowledge of fiction in the classroom and their insights into the tastes of their local clientele. The *Essex Review of Children's Literature* is one example of a local collaborative effort, looking at texts for the 4-15 age range. It is well worth subscribing—and then seeing if your cluster of schools or teachers' centre or adviser can get a similar enterprise on the move in your area, with your help.

School Librarian. S.L.A., Victoria House, 29-31 George Street, Oxford OX1 2AY.

A long-standing journal, known for its careful, independent reviewing of fiction from junior to 'A' levels. It also contains articles on the school library, lists forthcoming radio, film and television versions of books and gives details of articles on fiction and reading to be found in other journals. Four issues a year. There is a special membership rate for small schools.

Signal. Thimble Press, Station Road, South Woodchester, Stroud GL5 5EQ.

A journal with an international reputation, attracting a wide range of writers on its central topic of approaches to children's books. Three issues a year.

The Times Educational Supplement.

The *Times Ed* has reviews of children's fiction in most of its issues and quite often has articles on its use in school. It also produces special supplements on children's fiction, as does its sister publication *The Times Literary Supplement*. It is also worth looking at reviews of children's fiction in some of the daily and Sunday newspapers.

Use of English. Scottish Academic Press, 33 Montgomery Street, Edinburgh EH7 5JX.

This journal has long been a forum for all aspects of English teaching, with articles ranging from the philosophical to the very practical, including many on working with literature in secondary education. Some articles tackle specific texts, authors, genres, including work to 'A' level. Recommended.

4 Libraries

Bakewell K. *Classification and Indexing Practice*, Clive Bingley, 1978.

A useful overview of various ways of classifying a library as an efficient information source.

Dyer C. *School Libraries: Theory and Practice*, Clive Bingley, 1970.

A rigorous but interesting book, making helpful reading for anyone who has to argue for the central role of the library in a school—and for the proper uses of it!

Greenhalgh M. *Audiocassettes*, School Library Association, 1982.

A brief, practical, reasonably priced book on the selection, storage and use of audiocassettes, of particular use to anyone linking their book stocks with cassettes or starting a Listening Centre. Shrewd on what is available, with a useful list of suppliers of pre-recorded cassettes.

Hill, R. & Triggs. *How to Set Up and Run a School Bookshop.* School Bookshop Association, 1981.

A lively, practical guide to all aspects of setting up a bookshop, from designs for its furniture to how to attract and keep its customers. Well worth having a copy.

SLA Schools Sub-Committee. *SLA Guideline No 1: Routines—Managing a Small School Library*, School Library Association, 1980.

A very reasonably priced, commendably succinct book on the acquisition, cataloguing and storing of books and on the general running of a school library. Its useful appendices include information on suppliers of books and library equipment. Recommended.

Wehmeyer L. *The School Librarian as Educator*, Libraries Unlimited, Colorado, 1976.

A book for those interested in looking at other methods, showing in some details the more structured approaches to library use to be found in some schools in the U.S.A.

Winslade B. *Introduction to the Dewey Decimal Classification for British Schools* (3rd edn), School Library Association, 1977.

Since so many schools use some version of the Dewey System, this is worth having, perhaps as an inter-school investment.

5 Teaching

Calthrop K. *Reading Together: An Investigation into the Use of the Class Reader*, NATE/Heinemann Educational Books, 1971.

The report of an inquiry into the use of the class reader, suggesting that it can have much to commend it. The book gives several detailed, practical examples of how novels have been used across the age and ability range of the secondary school and provides lists of the most popular texts taught a decade ago. A useful and sensible book.

Centre for Children's Books. *Authors and Illustrators List*, Centre for Children's Books, London, 1981

A list of writers and illustrators who can be contacted through their publishers as speakers or visitors to schools. Worth consulting via your local library if you want to go beyond the range of people available through your Regional Arts Association's Writers in Schools scheme.

Chambers A. *Introducing Books to Children*, Heinemann Educational Books, 1973.

A sensible, enthusiastic book with many practical ideas for trying to ensure that pupils encounter books with pleasure. Sound advice on story telling and reading.

Foster J. (ed). *Reluctant to Read?*, Ward Lock Educational, 1978.

One of the few books to tackle the problem of the reluctant reader at secondary level, with some of its articles exploring the possible causes of reluctance and making suggestions about books and further approaches. See also Aidan Chambers's *The Reluctant Reader* (1969) for more ideas and Dan Fader's *Hooked on Books* (1966) and *The New Hooked on Books* (1976) for an

American view on how to help 'the poorest man', limited to his own experience, grow at least a little richer through reading.

Library Association Youth Libraries Group. *Storytelling,* Library Association Youth Libraries Group, London, 1979.

A collection of practical articles on storytelling and reading as means of sharing a text. John Ling's lively chapter on 'Putting on the Style' shows how a confident, well-organized promotion of books can be very effective.

Masterman M. *Teaching about Television,* Macmillan, 1980.

An introduction to using television in the classroom. Much of its focus is on television in its own right, but the book is also useful for the consideration of links with work on fiction.

Meek M. et al. *Achieving Literacy: Longitudinal Studies of Adolescents Learning to Read,* Routledge & Kegan Paul, 1983.

Important reading for anyone working with children who have failed to gain adequate literacy, with insights into readers and various teaching methods linked to detailed case studies.

Moody H. *The Teaching of Literature,* Longman, 1971.

A happy mixing of theory, insight and practice by a writer with experience of teaching overseas, providing the reader with a wide range of ideas.

Parker E. *Teaching the Reading of Fiction,* Teachers' College Press, New York, 1969.

An interesting book in its setting out a much more consciously structured and sequential approach than is usual in Britain.

Weiss M. & Lorac C. *Communication and Social Skills,* Wheaton, 1981.

An enthusiastic book, arguing that pupils should be makers of audiotape, tape-slide, videotape and film productions themselves as a means of exploring and communicating. Clearly of relevance to literary work, suggesting that such activities can be of particular benefit with the less able and the less motivated.

6 Teenagers

Carlsen G. *Books and the Teenage Reader,* Harper and Row, 1980.

Useful for its transatlantic perspective on adolescents and their reading and on what is provided for them in the U.S.A.

Heather P. *Young People's Reading: A Study of the Leisure Reading of 13-15 Year Olds,* CRUS, University of Sheffield, 1982.

A study of over fifty adolescents, their out of school reading and its links with their general social life and values.

Kennerley P. (ed). *Teenage Reading,* Ward Lock Educational, 1979.

An interesting collection of articles on teenagers' reading tastes, with implications for teaching strategies and tactics.

Marshall M. *Libraries and Literature for Teenagers,* Deutsch, 1975.

A sensible book on what influences teenagers in their reading—or non-reading—and what teachers and librarians can do about the gulf between what some teenagers want to read and what teachers and librarians want them to read.

Varlejs J. (ed). *Young Adult Literature in the Seventies,* Scarecrow Press, 1978.

An American book making a powerful case for YA (young adult!) fiction as distinct from children's fiction. The articles are varied, committed and sometimes contentious. Many of the novels mentioned are not available over here, but others are—by Zindel and Cormier, for instance—and it is interesting to get the American view on such work.

Whitehead F. et al. *Children and Their Books*. Macmillan, 1977.

This is the analysis of the Schools Council's *Children's Reading Habits 10-15 Project*, based on a survey carried out on eight thousand children in 1971. It raises some interesting issues, including the categorization of fiction into 'quality' and 'non-quality' and the perennial one of what makes certain books particularly popular while others fail to attract readers.

Appendix 7

Catalogues

This section contains details of catalogues in three parts, the first on publishers and booksellers and the second and third on suppliers and distributors of audio and visual materials.

Publishers' and booksellers' catalogues are one means of keeping up to date with fiction for the classroom or the library. You can obtain a full list of publishers of children's books from The Publishers' Association or in *Children's Books: An Information Guide*, published by the Centre for Children's Books.

The list printed here identifies some of the publishers and booksellers whose catalogues (**C**) are of interest to teachers working with pupils of eleven and upwards and whose publicity material (**P**) could help to enliven a classroom or library and attract pupils to books.

The list of suppliers of pre-recorded audio and video materials— cassettes, tapes and films—shows some of the range of resources available. Problems of cost, availability and, sometimes, suitability, can often be solved, especially where it is possible for teachers to pool their knowledge of materials and, perhaps, pool their hiring or purchase funds.

Addresses, phone numbers and postal charges may change. Most catalogues are free.

1 Publishers and booksellers

Armada See *William Collins*
Beaver Paperbacks
Beaver Publicity Department, Hamlyn Paperbacks, Astronaut House, Hounslow Road, Feltham TW14 9AR, 01-890 1480.

    C. Annotated, with some paperback fiction.
    P. Bookjackets, posters, etc. free of charge.
A. and C. Black Ltd
35 Bedford Row, London WC1R 4JH, 01-242 0946.

    C. Annotated and in full colour, with good range of young and picture books. Some multi-ethnic books.
    P. No charge.

Basil Blackwell Ltd
The Children's Bookshop, 6 Broad Street, Oxford OX1 3AU, 0865 4911.
> **C.** Very good annotated children's fiction catalogue as part of the shop's mail order service.

The Bodley Head
9 Bow Street, London WC2E 7AL, 01-836 9081.
> **C.** 'Books for New Adults' is one of the best annotated catalogues available. The list of books for the multi-racial community includes Dual-Language Picture Books (English and Greek/Italian/Gujarati/Turkish).
> **P.** Check what is available. Postage charge.

Books for Students Ltd
58–64 Berrington Road, Leamington Spa CV31 1BR, 0926 29341.
> **C.** Based on a stock of nine thousand titles. No annotation, but books placed in genres. Very useful additional 'specialist' booklists, e.g. 'Teenage Fiction Reading List', 'Popular Classics', 'Multi-Ethnic Books', 'Feminism', 'Redundancy', available on request.

Jonathan Cape Ltd
30 Bedford Square, London WC1B 3EL, 01-636 5764.
> **C.** Annotated—mainly for pre-twelve age range.

Chatto and Windus Ltd
40–42 William IV Street, London WC2N 4DF, 01-836 0127.
> **C.** Annotated list across the age range.

William Collins Sons and Co Ltd
14 St James's Place, London SW1A 1PS, 01-493 7070.
> **C.** Fontana Lions catalogue is among the best, with a full range of hardbacks and paperbacks from picture books to novels for older readers. Detailed annotation and illustration; thematic section; articles on authors, school bookshops, etc.
> **P.** Posters and information on most of the firm's authors available from the Children's Sales Promotions Manager. No charge.

J. M. Dent and Sons Ltd
Aldine House, 33 Welbeck Street, London W1M 8LX, 01-486 7233.
> **C.** Annotated. Some titles for secondary education levels.

Dragon Paperbacks
Granada Publishing Ltd, P.O. Box 9, 29 Frogmore, St Albans AL2 2NF, 0727 72727.
> **C.** Mainly for the young, with a few older titles.
> **P.** No charge.

Dobson Books Ltd
Brancepeth Castle, Durham DH7 8DF, 0385 780628.
> **C.** Annotated, with some teenage novels.

Faber and Faber Ltd
Children's Books Publicity, 3 Queen Square, London WC1N 3AU, 01-278 6881.

C. Well-annotated, very extensive list.

P. Notes on leading authors and artists, some bookjackets available. State age range and type of school. Small charge.

Fontana Lions See *William Collins*

Victor Gollancz Ltd

14 Henrietta Street, London WC2E 8QJ, 01-836 2006.

C. 'Gollancz Books for Children and Young Adults' catalogue is among the most extensive lists available. Well annotated, with reading and interest levels suggested. Some multi-ethnic titles.

P. Check with the firm.

Hamish Hamilton Children's Books

Garden House, 57–59 Long Acre, London WC2E 9JZ, 01-836 7733.

C. Well annotated, with a small but interesting senior fiction section.

P. Small charge.

Patrick Hardy Books

28 Percy Street, London W1P 9FF, 01-636 9166.

C. Small but interesting, well-annotated list including some young adult fiction.

P. Bookjackets as available.

Heffer's Children's Bookshop

30 Trinity Street, Cambridge CB2 1TB, 0223 358351.

C. Excellent annotated catalogue as part of the shop's mail order service. List of cassettes of children's fiction also available.

Heinemann Educational Books

22 Bedford Square, London WC1B 3HH, 01-637 3311.

C. The 'New Windmill Series' catalogue covers over 250 books from 10 to 'A' level under various headings. See also the 'Heinemann Secondary Readers' for fiction from Africa and the Caribbean; the 'Writing in Asia' and 'Favourite Stories' series; the 'Multi-Cultural Education' catalogue for the 'African Writers' and 'Caribbean Writers' series, suitable for older pupils.

William Heinemann Ltd

10 Upper Grosvenor Street, London W1X 9PA, 01-493 4141.

C. Annotated list of Heinemann Young Books. *Pyramid Books* are simple young adult fiction, often by quality writers.

P. Small charge.

Hodder and Stoughton Children's Books

P.O. Box 704, Dunton Green, Sevenoaks TN13 2YG, 0732 45011.

C. Some annotation. Much fiction, including picture books.

Hutchinson Junior Books

17–21 Conway Street, London W1P 5HL, 01-387 2811.

C. Annotated list, with some fiction for readers over twelve.

P. Bookjackets and posters as available. Small postage charge.

Kestrel Books
Kestrel Publicity Office, Penguin Books Ltd, 536 King's Road, London SW10 0UH, 01-351 2393.

C. One of the best annotated catalogues, with a very wide range of authors and some distinctive fiction for 14+ readers.

P. An imaginative and generous firm, with posters and bookjackets. Postage charge.

Knight Paperbacks See Hodder and Stoughton

Ladybird Books Ltd
P.O. Box 12, Beeches Road, Loughborough LE11 2NQ, 0509 68021.

C. Few comments except possible reading ages on series which pupils may have encountered in their early days with picture books.

Lion Paperbacks See *William Collins*

Longman Group Ltd
Longman House, Burnt Mill, Harlow CM20 2JE, 0279 26721.

C. Longman Young Books are described in the *Kestrel Books* catalogue. See also Longman's 'Secondary Schools English' catalogue: the 'Knockout' series is useful for its graded reading levels, the 'Imprint' series for fourth years and upwards. Cassettes are available for some of the 'Imprint' series.

Macmillan Children's Books
4 Little Essex Street, London WC2R 3LF, 01-836 6673.

C. Annotated, with likely reading ages.

P. Some jackets, posters and other material available. Postage charge.

Macmillan Education Ltd
4 Little Essex Street, London WC2R 3LF, 01-836 6633.

C. 'Club 75' catalogue for less able readers. 'Topliners' annotated catalogue is useful for young adult fiction, including some European texts in translation. Annotations include comment where a book's subject or treatment is controversial.

Methuen's Children's Books Ltd
11 New Fetter Lane, London EC4P 4EE, 01-583 9855.

C. Excellent, large catalogue, annotated and with reading and interest levels. Extensive range of books, from picture books and texts for reluctant readers to a senior fiction list. Pamphlet on books for the multi-racial classroom available.

P. Generous publicity material, including posters, bookjackets, stickers, etc. as available. Postage charge. Methuen can also be contacted for more information on their authors.

Oxford University Press
Children's Books Promotion Department, Walton Street, Oxford OX2 6DP, 0865 56767.

C. Children's Books catalogue provides a well-annotated, extensive quality list, ranging from some of the best picture books available to novels for older readers. Multi-Cultural Education booklist available.

P. Posters on Oxford children's authors. Postage charge.

Pan Books
Cavaye Place, London SW10 9PG, 01-373 6070.

C. *Piccolo* catalogue for readers up to fifteen.

P. Whatever happens to be available. No charge.

Penguin Books
Children's Marketing Department, 536 King's Road, London SW10 0UH, 01-351 2393.

C. The *Puffin* catalogue is one of the most extensive and usefully annotated available, including a thematic section and the *Puffin Plus* series for older readers. See also the very good 'Penguin Multi-Ethnic Booklist' by Rosemary Stones with independent reviews of young adult fiction and a useful list of organizations and further resources.

P. Good quality, usually including posters and bookjackets. Postage charge.

Piccolo Paperbacks See *Pan Books*
Puffin Books See *Penguin Books*
Scholastic Publications Ltd
141–143 Drury Lane, London WC2B 5TG, 01-379 7333.

C. 'Action' and 'Double Action' list of books written for American teenagers with reading problems.

2 Suppliers of records and audiocassettes

Argo Spoken Word Cassettes
Decca Records (U.K.), 50 New Bond Street, London W1Y 9HA.

A growing list of readings, ranging from *Black Beauty* and *The Jungle Book* to *Cold Comfort Farm* and *Nicholas Nickleby* as Dickens would have read it.

Chivers Sound and Vision
93–100 Locksbrook Road, Bath, Avon BA1 3HB, 0225 316872.

Essential, encyclopaedic catalogue, listing over two thousand cassettes ranging from books for the very young through to 'A' level. Extensive use of distinguished readers and many texts read un-abridged. An exciting range, worth departmental or library attention, especially if developing book-tape links.

Gower Publishing Co Ltd
Gower House, Croft Road, Aldershot, Hampshire GU11 3HR, 0252 331551.

Catalogue and pamphlets for the famous *Caedmon Spoken Word* series. Cassette readings of a very wide range of authors, sometimes by the writers themselves—fiction, young fiction, science fiction, drama, poetry.

Heffer's Children's Bookshop
30 Trinity Street, Cambridge CB2 1TB, 0223 358351.
   List of cassettes of children's fiction available.

Listen for Pleasure Club
Music for Pleasure Ltd, 1/3 Uxbridge Road, Hayes, Middlesex UB4 05Y.
   Growing list of children's titles available through retail outlets.

National Audio-Visual Aids Centre and Library
Paxton Place, Gipsy Road, London SE27 9SR.
   Useful catalogues, with material on fiction including legends and folk tales. Hiring service available.

3 Suppliers of film and videocassettes

Film hire can be expensive. Videocassette purchase can be the same. It is certainly worth pooling resources with other schools wherever you can. Many video catalogues contain only one or two titles which are versions of novels you are likely to use.

BBC Enterprises Ltd Film and Video Sales
Room 503, Villiers House, The Broadway, London W5 2PA, 01-743 5588.
   A disappointing catalogue as far as this book is concerned, given the BBC's distinguished record of televising novels. The Brontës, Sterne and Scott appear in their 'Writers' Houses' series.

British Film Institute
127 Charing Cross Road, London WC2H 0EA, 01-437 4355.
   Encyclopaedic catalogue (£4.50 at time of writing) entitled *Films and TV Drama on offer*, listing material offered for hire from all major companies. A very good starting-point for any search. The BFI also has its own Education Officer and its Film and Video Library, at 81 Dean Street, W1V 6AA (Telephone 01-734 6451), has videocassettes of broadcast television programmes for hire.

Rank Video
Rank AudioVisual Ltd, P.O. Box 70, Great West Road, Brentford TW8 9HR.
   Example of a commercial catalogue, with some relevant videos, such as *Great Expectations* among many which aren't. Such magazines as *VideoWorld* contain lists of the major pre-recorded videocassette producers and distributors.

Weston Woods Studios Ltd
14 Friday Street, Henley-on-Thames, Oxon RG9 1PZ, 04912 77033.
   Well-illustrated and annotated catalogue on audiovisual (film strip plus cassette) adaptations of famous books, mainly picture books for the young. Some material on how picture books are created.